LOOKING BACK AT BRITAIN

EXPANSION OF EMPIRE

1880s

EXPANSION OF EMPIRE

1880s

Brian Moynahan

Reader's Digest | gettyimages®

CONTENTS

1880s IMAGE GALLERY

FRONT COVER: A heavy breech-loading gun being lowered into position on its carriage with the aid of a steam-powered crane at the Royal Arsenal, Woolwich.

BACK COVER: A steam-powered submarine, *Resurgam II*, photographed in 1879. The submarine successfully completed trials, but was lost at sea in 1880, without loss of life, before she could be demonstrated to the Navy.

TITLE PAGE: Guests at a royal house party at Balmoral Castle in 1885.

OPPOSITE: Horse-drawn traffic on Piccadilly, looking west towards Hyde Park Corner, in about 1885.

FOLLOWING PAGES:

Dockers at the Royal Albert Docks in London loading up the *Arawa* in 1885. Like many ships of its day, the *Arawa* displays both funnels for steam-power and rigging for sails.

Two barefoot girls on rocks by the sea, photographed by Frank Meadow Sutcliffe in 1886.

The men of St Kilda, a remote island community some 40 miles west of the Outer Hebrides. The self-sufficient St Kildans became a tourist attraction in late-Victorian times, as intrepid sightseers made the rough crossing from the mainland to marvel at the islanders' isolated way of life and to buy their hand-crafted goods.

A coach-and-four stopped in the Pass of Melford near Oban in the West Highlands.

ROYAL ALBERT DOCKS "THE ARAWA" B. 1079.

QUEEN AND COUNTRY

Fifty years on from Victoria's accession to the throne, at her Golden Jubilee in 1887, both Queen and country were all but unrecognisable. The population of Britain had doubled. The number living in the big towns and cities was now greater than those in the country. The one in five people who had lived in towns of 5,000 or more at the beginning of the century were to become four in five by its end. The example of Middlesbrough was striking but not unusual: from a hamlet of 25 souls, it had grown to a town of 46,000.

CELEBRATION Crowds even perched on rooftops to get a glimpse of Queen Victoria's carriage in the Golden Jubilee procession from Westminster Abbey on 22 June, 1887.

THE GOLDEN JUBILEE

The Queen herself was changed utterly. The slight teenager who had begun her reign so long before had become a reassuring symbol of permanence in a world of madcap change. Victoria had grown plump, and dowdy, dressed in black in memory of a husband long dead – 'dropsical', one newspaper said, 'somewhat unwieldy, and unable to stand on her legs'.

Those legs were short, so much so, *Photographic News* revealed, that she stood on a hidden box when photographed in her robes to increase her height. But she was every inch a Queen-Empress, nonetheless, mistress of a superpower and the greatest empire since Rome. She had given her name to the age, as her country had given the world Greenwich as its prime meridian of longitude in 1884, and Greenwich Mean Time as its standard time.

Assassination target

It was hard to imagine with Golden Jubilee celebrations in full swing, but Victoria's people had not always loved her. For years after Albert's death she had been a distant figure, rarely seen in London, holing herself up with her grief at Windsor Castle or on her estates in the Highlands of Scotland and on the Isle of Wight. 'A name', *The Times* had written, 'rather than a living reality.'

There had been eight attempts to assassinate her, the most recent in 1882. A would-be Scottish poet, Roderick Maclean, had fired a shot from a revolver into her carriage at Windsor railway station, before he was overpowered by the crowd. Victoria's response was splendidly cool and regal. 'Brown brought the revolver for me to see', she wrote in her diary, Brown being her Highland servant and confidant, 'I saw the bullets.' Maclean was tried for high treason, and sent to an asylum as 'not guilty but insane'. The wording irritated the Queen and as a result an act was passed changing such verdicts to 'guilty but insane'.

The public had made little of previous attempts on her life. This one, though, provoked a fresh sense of affection for the doughty monarch. Maclean's fellow Scot and would-be poet, William McGonagall, indefatigable writer of doggerel, caught the mood in the following lines:

> God prosper our noble Queen,
> And long may she reign!
> Maclean he tried to shoot her,
> But it was all in vain.
>
> Maclean must be a madman,
> Which is obvious to be seen,
> Or else he wouldn't have tried to shoot
> Our most beloved Queen.

continued on page 18

THE PUBLIC FACE
Victoria had come to the throne at the age of just 18. This formal photograph, taken to mark her Golden Jubilee in 1887, reflects the weight of the intervening half a century. She had borne four sons and five daughters in 21 years of marriage. She had been widowed, and her children went on to occupy the thrones of Europe. She had become Empress of India, as well as Queen. She had so marked the era that it bore her name: the Victorian Age.

After the death of her husband, Prince Albert, the Queen spent so much time at Windsor Castle – seen below in a view from across the Thames – that she became known as 'the widow of Windsor'. The stylish boats moored in the foreground were for hire by excursionists to row up and down the river. This was a bustling and physical age.

OUTBURSTS OF DISCONTENT

An attempt on the Queen's life at Windsor railway station in March 1882, depicted in an artist's sketch. A Scotsman called Roderick Maclean had sent Victoria a loyal address. He saw the polite but formal reply as an insult to his poetic talents and vowed vengeance. He fired one shot from his revolver into her carriage, missed, and was overpowered before he could shoot again. It was the eighth attempt on Victoria's life. The first had been in 1840, when she was pregnant with her first child: 18-year-old Edward Oxford fired twice into her carriage and missed. He and Maclean were both found insane. Two more attempts came within three months of each other in 1842. The only injury to her person was in 1850, when an ex-Army officer struck her with his cane, causing bruising and crushing her bonnet. He failed to prove himself insane, and was sentenced to transportation.

VICTORIA'S LONG JOURNEY

A commemorative souvenir picture (below) shows two paintings of Queen Victoria, at the start of her reign in 1837 and at the time of the Golden Jubilee, with drawings of Windsor Castle and Balmoral. Huge crowds greeted her (right) as she drove through Trafalgar Square at the high point of the celebrations. Irish anarchists had been foiled in their attempt to blow up the thanksgiving service in Westminster Abbey.

The country itself was unrecognisable from the quieter, more rural realm it had been at her accession. The population had doubled, with the number living in the big towns and cities now far greater than those in the country. The infant railways had become Titans, and there were other new marvels aplenty: anaesthetics, the telegraph and telephone, the electric light bulb, the lightweight camera, the safety bicycle, and – of importance to an Empire that was acquiring new territory at an average rate of 100,000 square miles a year – the Maxim machine gun and the all-iron warship.

Happier creations of the reign included football, rugby and lawn tennis, and the codifications of their rules. There were now cricket Test matches as the sport was enthusiastically taken up around the empire, and the FA Cup competition to thrill crowds at home. Innumerable civic buildings that are still in use today – the Houses of Parliament, our great Town Halls, concert halls, national museums, and church and village halls up and down the land – were built in this Victorian half century.

Affection and honours

By the time of her Golden Jubilee, in June 1887, the feeling had matured into what she described, with a touching sense of surprise, as the 'marvellous kindness, loyalty and devotion of so many millions, which really I could hardly have expected'. The souvenir manufacturers sensed that this was to be a special year. On New Year's Day, the Prince of Wales gave his mother a Jubilee inkstand, the first off the production line. 'It was shaped like the crown, which opened, and on the inside there is a head of me', Victoria wrote. 'It is very pretty and useful.'

The first general awards of honours were made, as 'New Year' and 'Birthday honours', with record numbers of new peerages. 'God Save the Queen' was played so often that Lady Randolph Churchill announced that she had bought a dress from the couturier Worth that played the anthem every time she sat down. In fact, she had a young man concealed under her couch with a musical box.

TRAGIC LOSS OF A SON-IN-LAW

Frederick, the German Crown Prince, the only son of Kaiser Wilhelm I, was thought to be the most impressive of the many relations who attended the Queen's Jubilee. He was married to the Princess Royal and known as 'Fritz' to Victoria, his mother-in-law. He was a powerful military figure, resplendent in his uniform as a field marshal who had commanded an army in the Franco-Prussian war in 1870. But the experience had given Frederick a horror of the waste of war, for he was a thoughtful man who disliked militarism and the autocratic ideas that dominated Prussia. He protested against Bismarck's attacks on constitutional rights and the press. He strove, wherever possible, to liberalise Germany's institutions.

The Prince was suffering from a growth in his throat. German specialists had diagnosed cancer and planned an operation to surgically remove the prince's larynx. Frederick was also seen by Morell Mackenzie (right), one of the pioneers of laryngology with a formidable reputation. Victorian science was highly international, and Mackenzie had studied in Paris, Vienna and Budapest as well as at the London Hospital. He was largely responsible for the foundation of the Throat Hospital in King Street in London. Mackenzie examined the Prince and found no evidence that the affected tissue was cancerous. The growth might well be benign, he said, and the planned operation was not justifiable. Frederick travelled to London for the Jubilee, seeing Mackenzie again before going on to Balmoral. Mackenzie was rewarded for his opinion with a knighthood in September 1887, and with the Grand Cross of the Hohenzollern Order. But in November, the German doctors were again consulted. They remained of the opinion that the growth was cancerous.

Wilhelm I died in March the following year and the Crown Prince succeeded him as Frederick III, King of Prussia and Emperor of Germany. Just three months later, in June 1888, Frederick followed his father to the grave, while the argument still raged between Mackenzie and the German specialists. Frederick's death has historic echoes, as it robbed Germany of a moderate and modest ruler at a crucial time. He was succeeded by his son, Wilhelm II, who was everything his father was not: a militarist and Anglophobe who thought his grandmother 'an old hag'. But that brooding menace was for the future.

The Queen had visited Birmingham in March, to lay the foundations of the new law courts. *The Times* estimated that half a million people came out to cheer her, many of them from 'the roughest classes of population in England'. She was particularly touched by the warmth of her reception in Liverpool in May. The one sour note came that same month, when she visited London's East End. There, she told Lord Salisbury, she heard 'a horrid noise', quite new to her ear – 'booing', she believed it was called. Her Prime Minister responded that 'all that is worthless, worn out or penniless naturally drifts to London', and should not be taken seriously. The booing, he was sure, came from socialists or the Irish, 'very resentful men who would stick at nothing to show their fury'. Irish MPs voted against assigning £18,000 for decorating Westminster Abbey for the Jubilee. More threateningly, a five-man cell of Fenians smuggled explosives into Britain, planning to bomb the thanksgiving service in the Abbey, but the special police branch dealing with Irish terrorism was tipped off and the plot aborted.

For the rest, the country basked in the Jubilee. The small West Country village of Christon was one of the first off the mark. The whole village of 80 souls enjoyed beef and mutton in a local farmer's wagon shed at the beginning of May. Loxton, in Somerset, had two celebrations. At the end of May, Major Erasmus Galton, the lord of the manor, gave a lunch for 100 of his tenants and their families. In the afternoon, sports and games were played in the orchard until tea, and after tea they danced until darkness fell.

At the climax of the Jubilee, on June 21, the rector of Loxton, J G Tiarks, hosted a service at noon, bells pealing, the church festooned in flags. Rev Tiarks then gave a lunch for 30 of his tenants and friends. In the evening, the parishioners entered the rectory grounds in procession, singing the National Anthem and waving flags. The rector took a group photograph, and dancing and refreshments were followed by the lighting of a beacon on a nearby hill.

Victoria's big day

The Queen had started her celebration the day before, breakfasting quietly under the trees at Frogmore, resting place of Prince Albert. She then travelled by train from Windsor to Paddington, crossing the parks to Buckingham Palace. A royal banquet was held that evening. There were 50 foreign kings and princes in attendance, but it was, as she wrote in her diary, 'a large family dinner'. As an observer noted, she was 'mother and mother-in-law and grandmother of all that regal company ...'

'Never, never can I forget this brilliant year ...'

Queen Victoria, on the year of her Golden Jubilee

The party assembled in the Bow Room, then dined – on fillets of beef, whole chickens, lobsters, ducks, venison steaks, pastries and cakes – at a large horseshoe table in the supper room. 'The King of Denmark took me in', Victoria wrote, 'and Willy of Greece sat on my other side. The Princes were all in uniform, and the Princesses were all beautifully dressed. Afterwards we went into the Ballroom, where my band played.'

Next day, the Queen went to Westminster Abbey in an open landau. She refused to wear a crown, and the spectators packed on benches suspended along 10 miles of scaffolding saw a plump little old lady in a black satin dress, with a bonnet trimmed with white lace, escorted by brilliantly uniformed Indian cavalry. The procession, Mark Twain observed, 'stretched to the limit of sight on both sides'. He noted the many Indian princes, 'men of stately build and princely carriage', in turbans flashing with rubies and diamonds. They glistened like jewels, the Maharajahs of Cutch and Indore winning special cheers as they passed. The European royalty was sombre by comparison. As for the Queen, Twain recorded 'she was like a little old lady coming to church to thank God …'

After the thanksgiving service at the Abbey, the Queen returned to the Palace, besieged by huge crowds who cheered her when she appeared on the balcony. She distributed Jubilee brooches to her family. In the evening she attended a banquet wearing a splendid patriotic gown embroidered with roses, thistles and shamrocks. Afterwards, she received diplomats and Indian princes before being wheeled in her chair to watch fireworks in the garden. On New Year's Eve, she wrote in her diary: 'Never, never can I forget this brilliant year …' Her people, 50 years on, had come to love her. Or most of them. Not the Irish, or at least not the non-Ulster Irish.

PARTY POLITICS AND REFORM

The 1880s were dominated by the Irish question. It split the Liberal party, with breakaway Liberal Unionists joining the Conservatives, driving from office the great champion of Irish Home Rule, William Gladstone. It split Ireland, too, into North and South, and the failure to solve it led to the sporadic outbursts of violence that have continued into our own age. The bombs that Fenians set at London's mainline railway stations in February 1884 were the direct antecedents of IRA explosions a century later.

Other political reforms took place in the decade, with greater success. Modern constituencies and our system of local government date from this decade. Parliamentary candidates were already required to publish their election expenses. The Corrupt Practices Act of 1883 set limits and controls, and the amount of spending fell dramatically. The outright bribery of electors, once commonplace, became so rare that no successful claims of bribery were made at the next general election. The power of the political parties also increased. Rich individuals could no longer rely on their money to win them a seat. The importance of the party machine and the constituency agent was on the rise. There were more MPs of modest means and orthodox party views, and fewer independents.

Electoral reform
The electorate as defined by the second Reform Act of 1867 had reached 3 million by 1884. That year, Gladstone introduced a third Reform Act which raised it again to 5.6 million, bringing in large numbers of new voters in the county seats. Two thirds of adult men in England and Wales now had the vote, and three fifths of Scots. The biggest change was in Ireland, where the electorate shot up from 225,000 to almost 750,000 and half the men now had the vote.

In terms of MPs, though, Scotland and Ireland were over-represented compared to England and Wales. Seats were redistributed on modern lines the

POLITICAL PROGRESS

Much of our modern political system solidified during the decade. In 1883, the Corrupt and Illegal Practices Act set limits and controls on the election expenses of parliamentary candidates. As a result, the outright bribery of electors all but disappeared. Rich individuals could no longer buy seats. In 1844, Gladstone introduced the Representation of the People Bill. It passed through the House of Commons, where the Liberals had a majority, but was rejected by the Lords. Mass demonstrations were held in protest (above) and a crowd of more than 80,000 gathered in Hyde Park that October. The Lords passed the Act in December, after the Tories were promised that constituencies would also be reformed. Two men in three now had the vote. The Redistribution Act duly followed in June 1885. This established the modern type of single member constituency. Representation was made fairer, as the number of people and voters in big towns was at last reflected in the number of seats. The influence of the parties, and of the House of Commons, was greatly increased. That of the Lords diminished, with government increasingly run from the lower house.

RE-DRAWING THE POLITICAL MAP
Horse-drawn trams in Piccadilly in the heart of Manchester. Following the Redistribution Act of 1885, big cities like Manchester were at last allotted sufficient seats in Parliament to reflect the size of the population. Manchester now had six MPs, as did Sheffield; Liverpool had nine, Birmingham seven and Leeds four. The number of MPs in London all but tripled, from 22 to 62.

The city of Manchester might no longer be quite the 'Cottonopolis' it had once been, as mills were opened in Bolton and Oldham, but it was at its dynamic height around the 1880s. Many of its municipal buildings, including the magnificent Town Hall, were under construction or completed. The Hallé Orchestra enhanced the city's cultural profile, while its banks and insurance companies were giving it status as the financial capital of the North. And the Manchester Ship Canal was under construction: within a few years, this would open to allow ocean-going ships to dock right in the city, bringing supplies to its new chemical and engineering industries.

following year. An MP no longer represented a town or a community, often in tandem with another MP. With a few exceptions, he now sat for a specific, single-member, geographically separate constituency. The character of constituencies in party terms – whether they were 'safe' or 'marginal' – now became established depending on their social composition. South Kensington, for example, was safely Conservative, Lambeth safely Liberal (later Labour).

Seventy-nine towns with fewer than 15,000 people lost their borough status and their MPs, as they were merged into their counties. Thirty-six more towns with populations under 50,000 lost one of their MPs. In a few middle-sized cities, like Bradford, Hull and Stockport, the old pattern continued, with the town as a whole electing two or three MPs. The large cities all gained more MPs, as the number allotted was adjusted to reflect their populations.

New County Councils

The County Councils Act of 1888 replaced the Justices of the Peace, the magistrates who had run the old shires, with 62 new elected county councils. Sixty-one towns with over 50,000 people were given county borough status. London got its own county council, the LCC, carved out of the urban areas of Middlesex, Surrey, Essex and Kent, and would soon have a global reputation for enlightened city government.

The big cities had been given elected corporations more than 50 years before. The shires, though, had remained in the hands of the JPs. With the extension of the vote to many more electors in the shires, reform was overdue. In practice, at least in England, many JPs were elected to the new county councils, and the lords-lieutenants became chairmen. The Welsh were less deferential. Nonconformist Liberals were elected in great numbers, at the expense of the gentry. An equivalent act for Scotland was passed in 1889.

The right to affirm

Freedom of conscience for MPs was established after the 1880 election in the true British manner – grudgingly, slowly, but granted nonetheless. The driving force was Charles Bradlaugh, who was elected that year in Northampton. Bradlaugh's father was a lawyer's clerk, his mother a nursemaid, and he had grown up to be a secularist, radical and republican, who signed his pamphlets 'Iconoclast' and supported the nationalist aspirations of the Irish, Poles and Italians. As an avowed atheist, he wanted to affirm rather than swear the oath required of sitting MPs, as was already allowed in law courts. The Tories made much of a non-believer in the

TWO RADICALS
Charles Bradlaugh (above) was a key figure in establishing freedom of conscience for Members of Parliament. A one-time errand boy, coal merchant and soldier, he became owner-editor of the *National Reformer* and a powerful speaker. An athiest, he refused to take the MP's oath of allegiance and was expelled from Parliament, whereupon the electors of Northampton re-elected him. This time he offered to take the oath, but in a letter to *The Times* he wrote that an oath in the name of a God he did not believe in meant nothing. He was expelled again – and elected again. He was eventually allowed to take his seat in 1886. Two years later, affirmation of the oath became legal.

The remarkable Annie Besant (right) separated from her clergyman husband to become vice-president of the National Secular Society. She was charged with obscenity after publishing a pamphlet on birth control. She was also a prominent member of the Fabian Society, whose aim was to propagate socialism by non-revolutionary means. Having shocked Britain, she moved to India, where she went into pro-independence politics. At the age of 70, in 1917, the old firebrand became president of the Indian National Congress.

Liberal ranks. Gladstone, though he despised Bradlaugh's views, defended his right to hold them, but the views of Tory firebrands like Lord Randolph Churchill and A J Balfour held sway. The Commons rejected Bradlaugh – a 'seditious blasphemer', said Churchill, propped up by 'mob scum and dregs'. The good voters of Northampton disagreed and duly re-elected him.

Bradlaugh was about to become even more controversial. In 1886, with the equally radical Annie Besant, he brought out an edition of an American book in favour of birth control. The government prosecuted for 'depraving public morals', and Bradlaugh was briefly imprisoned before the sentence was quashed on a technicality. The voters of Northampton returned him yet again. He was at length allowed to take his seat, and affirmation of the oath was made legal in 1888. These were important reforms. For the rest, though, prime ministers and parliament were caught up in Ireland.

Disraeli's end

The decade began with Benjamin Disraeli apparently comfortable in power. Not long before, the Conservative Prime Minister had conferred the title of Empress of India on the Queen and she had raised him to the peerage as Earl of Beaconsfield.

William Gladstone, Disraeli's predecessor as Prime Minister and long-standing Liberal rival, had resigned as party leader in 1874 and appeared to be chasing phantoms. He reacted furiously when in 1876 Muslim tribal irregulars murdered a thousand Christians in a village church in Turkish-ruled Bulgaria. He dashed off a pamphlet entitled *The Bulgarian Horrors and the Question of the East*. His oratory was still masterful, if overblown. 'Let the Turks now carry away their abuses', he raged, 'by carrying off themselves, their Bimbashis and Yuzbachis, their Kaimakans and their Pashas, one and all, bag and baggage, and clear out from the province that they have desolated and profaned. This thorough riddance, this most blessed deliverance, is the only reparation we can make to those heaps and heaps of dead, the violated purity alike of matron and of maiden and of child; to the civilization which has been affronted and shamed; to the laws of God, or, if you like, of Allah ... There is not a criminal in a European jail, there is not a criminal in the South Sea Islands, whose indignation would not rise and over-boil ...'

There was one person who remained distinctly underwhelmed and unruffled, and that was Benjamin Disraeli. Even in full moral flow – or as Disraeli put it, 'inebriated with the exuberance of his own verbosity' – Gladstone did not miss a political trick. The Queen called him 'that half madman' and found him 'most reprehensible and mischievous'. Disraeli largely ignored the events in Bulgaria, even though it was just the sort of issue 'to drive John Bull mad' – 'a good dose of Cross and Crescent, plus Civilization versus Barbarism'.

But Gladstone's moral and religious passion caught a spirit of the age. Disraeli might mock his pamphlet, but it sold 200,000 copies in little more than a month. A crowd of 10,000 flocked to hear Gladstone at Blackheath. The Grand Old Man was back, even though he was now 70 and had first been elected an MP almost 50 years before. He had decided early in 1879 to stand at the next election for Midlothian, the Scottish county that surrounds Edinburgh, where he campaigned with extraordinary vigour against Disraeli and 'Beaconsfieldism'.

Disraeli was old, and sick, and over-confident. The Conservatives seemed strong. They had won two by-elections that the Liberals had hopes of winning. They had a 100-seat majority over the Liberals and 50 seats over Liberals and Irish Home Rulers combined. In March 1880, Disraeli went to the Queen and asked her to dissolve Parliament early. His timing was not good. The electorate was out of sorts after the worst winter of the century. Taxes had risen to pay for foreign adventures. Farming was in a slump. Land values were on the slide. Industry was in the doldrums. Gladstone's Midlothian speeches were pulling crowds of many thousands as he pounded out national policies from the stump.

It was a Liberal landslide. They won 353 seats, up by more than 100, while the Tories slumped from 351 to 238. The Irish Home Rulers had 61 seats: Gladstone had a working majority without them and was triumphant.

Disraeli, the great adventurer and inventor of one-nation Toryism, was gone from power. A year later he was dead. The Queen's grief – 'the loss is so overwhelming' – was compounded by her abiding dislike of Gladstone, now back from retirement, as energetic and distasteful to her as ever. She tried to persuade Lord Hartington to form a ministry, but was obliged to bow to the inevitable.

DISRAELI BOWS OUT
If ever two men naturally loathed one another, it was the two towering figures of mid-Victorian politics: the Tory Benjamin Disraeli (above) and the Liberal William Gladstone. Disraeli was a rare and exotic figure for a Tory leader. He was a master debater, a skilful parliamentary operator and a great favourite of the Queen. He had a 'power of saying in two words that which drives a person of Mr Gladstone's peculiar temperament into a great state of excitement'. But Disraeli lost the 1880 election to Gladstone, who revelled in his old rival's defeat. The following year, two weeks before he died, an acquaintance visited Disraeli to find him lying exhausted on a couch. But he found that the former leader 'was still the old Disraeli, and, though I think he knew that he was dying, yet his pleasant spitefulness about Mr G was not abated'. Mr G, of course, was Gladstone, who the next day noted in his diary of his opponent: 'May the Almighty be near his pillow.'

THE PROBLEMS OF IRELAND

Gladstone's second administration lasted for five years from June 1880: for two of them, the tireless workhorse was Chancellor of the Exchequer as well as Prime Minister. Ireland would be his undoing.

Ireland had been confirmed as a part of the United Kingdom by the Act of Union of 1800. Sending its own MPs to the Westminster Parliament, it appeared to be in the same situation as Scotland, whose own Union with England and Wales had taken place a century earlier. But Ireland was always unlike the mainland nations, and it grew more so with time. It was overwhelmingly rural, its people scattered in small villages and isolated cottages. Its largest class were impoverished native tenant farmers and peasants, at odds with the smallest, the Anglo-Irish landlords of the old Protestant Ascendancy. A farmer was classified as 'rich' if he had 80 acres or more and 'snug' if he had 50 acres. These accounted for little more than one in ten. The great majority were landless labourers and 'cottiers', who rented a few acres and a cottage from a farmer, paying with work in the fields.

There was little industry, apart from linen and engineering and shipbuilding in Belfast. Many Ulstermen were Scots in origin and Presbyterian in religion, making them quite distinct from the provinces to the south. Four in five Irish were Catholics, with the remaining fifth of the population about evenly divided between Presbyterians of various sorts and Anglicans of the Church of Ireland.

The population surge from the 1740s onwards had been the greatest in Europe. Only England and Finland came close. By the early 1840s, despite the loss of 1.3 million to emigration since Waterloo, 8.3 million people were living in Ireland. In comparison England, with its greater land area and infinitely more advanced industry, had barely 15 million to support.

By then, the first large-scale movement to repeal the Union had flowered under Daniel O'Connell, and wilted. Through peaceful mass protest and the influence of the Catholic clergy, O'Connell succeeded in winning Catholic emancipation – from 1829, for the first time since the Reformation, Roman Catholics were allowed to sit in the British Parliament. This did nothing for the Irish poor, though: Mr O'Connell and rich Catholics might go to Westminster, but that did not feed the hungry. Though he was called 'the liberator', he was himself a Kerry property owner, who mistrusted revolutionary nationalism and disliked violence. In 1843 agitation to repeal the Union reached a height, but the Duke of Wellington poured 35,000 troops into the island, O'Connell abandoned a great meeting planned at Clontarf and the moment passed. In 1847 O'Connell was dead, the potato famine struck and Home Rule remained beyond reach.

The Irish diaspora and fate of those left behind

Since then, Ireland had suffered a population collapse on a terrifying scale illuminated by this simple statistic. When Victoria came to the throne, the Irish accounted for some 30 per cent of the UK population. By the time of her Golden Jubilee that figure was down to 12.5 per cent, a fall without parallel in Europe. The famine deaths during the years of the potato blight accounted for about 1.1 million. A further 2.1 million had emigrated. Poor harvests now threatened a

WOMAN OF GALWAY
A woman in County Galway balances a basket of fish on her head, at a time when the hard-won bounty of the sea was not matched by the meagre pickings from the soil. By 1880 life in the west of Ireland, after a brief respite following the Great Famine, was desperate once more. The potato crop failed for several successive harvests after 1877. Outbreaks of disease decimated pigs and poultry. Prices for butter were falling. Seasonal jobs in fishing and harvesting slumped. Smallholders were pushed into penury. Those who could sailed away on the emigrant boats to Britain, America, Australia and New Zealand.

repeat of that dreadful catastrophe. In the 1880s the island was haemorrhaging people at a faster rate than at any time since the famine. Emigrants left for Liverpool and Glasgow, or to America and Australia, where the Irishmen already there were Anglophobes, willing to fund violent campaigns for independence.

As for those who remained, a *Telegraph* journalist, in Connemara in January 1880, saw what he took to be a pile of rubbish at the side of the road, a mound with smoke drifting from it. Then a woman emerged from the pile, with a baby at her breast. On the coast, the entrance to a cave in the cliff was stopped up with a lobster pot. It, too, was inhabited. Tenants, ruined as food prices fell, were evicted under the harsh tenets of 'landlordism'.

Prime Ministers rarely visited this strange and hostile place. Disraeli and Salisbury never went there. The Queen spent just five weeks of her long reign there. Even Gladstone, so attached to the rights of the poor and oppressed, agreed that the strain of violence on the island merited exceptional measures. In 1881 he saw through a fresh Irish Coercion Act, which permitted the Viceroy in Dublin to detain people for as 'long as was thought necessary'.

Parnell and Home Rule

By now, the Home Rulers had a new leader. Irish nationalism was never a Catholic monopoly. It had Protestant Anglo-Irish leaders and sympathisers, for all the hostility of the Scots Presbyterians of Ulster. Charles Stewart Parnell was exactly what the Catholic peasantry might be expected most to detest. He was a young Protestant landlord from County Wicklow, with impeccable Establishment

HIDDEN SKILL
Poteen, illegally distilled potato whiskey, being made in Connemara in 1885. The excisemen were constantly on the look-out for stills, but the country was large and stills easily moved. Poteen ranged from fiery rotgut to a fine peaty-flavoured spirit given extra zest by being banned – and tax-free.

THE MALL. CORK. 814.

LAST VIEW OF HOME

The harbour in Cork, Ireland's second city, in the early 1880s, a peak period for emigrants. For many of those leaving, their last glimpse of the Old World was of this waterfront, as they sailed away for North America or began the long voyage round the globe to Australia and New Zealand.

About 3.25 million people emigrated from Britain and Ireland during the decade, an astonishingly high figure that far outstripped the combined total from Germany and Italy, the other two countries in Europe with sizeable numbers of emigrants. Rather less than a quarter of emigrants from the British Isles went to Canada or Australia. More than

two thirds went to the United States. The telegraph and a hugely improved postal service were making the links between English-speaking peoples around the world ever closer. Australia was no longer almost as remote as the moon. In just one month in 1881, more than 3 million letters and parcels arrived from there.

credentials. His great-grandfather had been chancellor of the Irish Exchequer, he was Cambridge-educated, he rode to hounds, he adored cricket and he dressed for dinner – not things that would endear him to Fenians.

In broad terms, Parnell wanted to win for Ireland the same dominion status as Canada or Australia. The Union would go, but the island would remain part of the British Empire, with its own parliament and self-government. London had shown itself only too pleased to see the big white colonies rule themselves – it was cheaper and less bother. This should be even more true of Ireland. But details were vague and important questions were left hanging. Who would appoint the police and judges? Would Irish MPs continue to sit at Westminster? Would London be responsible for foreign policy and for waging war, as in the other dominions?

The lack of precision combined with Parnell's personal charisma allowed most of the Irish nation – hardliners and soft, peasants and moderate landowners – to gather behind him. He won the support of the Catholic clergy, despite being a Protestant. It was a vital factor, for the hold of the clergy had been strengthened by the loss of population: the size of the average congregation was half what it had been before the Famine, giving the priest greater intimacy and influence.

The Land League and Land War

Discontent in the countryside was led by the Land League. It was started with funds from America by Michael Davitt, a veteran of Fenian outrages in England in the 1860s, who had served time in Dartmoor for gun-running. The League

RELIGION AND MINING

The haunting monastic site of Glendalough in Co Wicklow had been a place of pilgrimage for more than a thousand years. St Kevin – a member of the royal house of Leinster who had turned to solitariness and poverty – lived in a nearby cave as a hermit. After his death in the early 7th century, his followers founded a monastery which thrived until the dissolution of the Irish monasteries under Henry VIII. In the 1880s Irish Catholic pilgrims were still coming to this church, known as St Kevin's Kitchen because its belfry resembles a chimney. It had been revived as a place of worship in the early 19th century, and the ancient Round Tower in the background had recently been restored.

Lead, copper, zinc and silver had long been worked by the Mining Company of Ireland at Glendalough. Up to 2,000 worked in the mines, but they were now being run down. Mining ceased completely by the end of the decade.

6625. CO. WICKLOW, ST. KEVINS KITCHEN & ROUND TOWER, GLENDALOUGH.   L.S.&P.C.

TWO FACES OF NATIONALISM
There were two strains to Irish nationalism.
One was broadly-based, open, in favour of
pressure but not outright violence. The
other was secretive, violent, trading in
terror and assassination. At the peak of his
powers, Charles Stewart Parnell (left),
pictured in 1885, managed to sustain a
unity that embraced both wings of the
cause. He was a Protestant, a landowner
and grandson of the chancellor of the Irish
Exchequer. Such impeccable Establishment
credentials should have been anathema to
a gun-runner like Michael Davitt (above), a
peasant's son hailing originally from Co
Mayo, and a Fenian who had been
sentenced to 15 years for shipping guns to
Ireland in 1870. Davitt began an anti-
landlord crusade, and was again
imprisoned in 1881 for breaking the
conditions of his early release. For most of
the decade, Parnell was able to hold
together the many strands of nationalists:
ultra-conservative Catholic bishops,
would-be social revolutionaries, rural
hotheads, impoverished peasants, as well
as idealistic Protestants like himself.

threatened those who crossed it with visits by 'Captain Moonlight'. Tenants who
were thought submissive to their landlords, and hostile to the League, could find
their ricks burning, their cattle maimed, their barns and houses set on fire, always
at night. Davitt was imprisoned and Parnell elected president of the Land League.

The violence in the so-called 'Land War' began in Connacht. It spread to reach
a peak in the year to mid-June 1882. If a tenant was evicted, no-one could take on
the farm, on pain of being 'isolated from his kind as if he were a leper of old'. This
is exactly what happened when a land agent, Captain Boycott, took over a farm in
Co Mayo. He was met with angry, cursing men who refused to work or trade or
talk with him, and the word 'boycott' entered the language.

When another much-hated land agent died, bonfires were lit on the hills: 'over
a district of upwards of 20,000 acres there was scarcely a mile without a bonfire
blazing in manifests of joy at his decease'. Samuel Hussey, land agent and farmer,
was thought 'the most abused man in Ireland'. His house was attacked with
dynamite in 1884. 'I never travelled without a revolver and occasionally a
Winchester rifle', he wrote. 'I used to place my revolver beside my fork at the
dinner table as I spread my napkin on my knee.'

THE MURDER OF INNOCENCE AT PHOENIX PARK

On 6 May, 1882, Lord Frederick Cavendish (above) and Thomas Burke (above right) were walking through Phoenix Park in Dublin when they were set upon and cut to pieces by a gang of men wielding surgical knives. Burke was the most senior Irish civil servant of the day. Cavendish was the amiable younger brother of the Duke of Devonshire and barely off the boat as the new Irish Secretary.

The butchery produced deep shock. When Gladstone and his wife heard the news, they 'threw themselves on their knees in the inner hall, and as soon as they had partially recovered themselves, they at once set out for Lady Frederick's'. The Queen told Gladstone a little later that the style of the murders was 'calculated to make one's blood run cold and to produce an indescribable thrill of horror'. Parnell went 'white as a sheet, agitated and apparently altogether demoralised'. Afraid that he would be next, he took to carrying a revolver in his overcoat when he was at Westminster.

The murders produced a feeling of the loss of innocence. Life in Victorian Britain was often brutal, sometimes violent, but for politicised criminality to intrude on public life in such a vicious way was a sickening blow to national self-respect. Years later, the liberal reformer Violet Markham, a young girl at the time, could still recall her mother's 'face of horror' as she hurried up the garden path to tell her father of the news. 'The moral sense of the times had not been blunted by the large-scale cruelties and horrors of two world wars.'

The assassins were Fenian extremists who called themselves 'the Invincibles'. Arrests were soon made. Five men were convicted of the murders and hanged in Kilmainham jail.

The Phoenix Park murders and a change in public mood

'Captain Moonlight' also dug graves by the houses of 'traitors'. They were not filled yet, but on 6 May, 1882, two murders took place in Dublin that shocked even Fenians. Lord Frederick Cavendish, the recently appointed Irish Secretary, was walking in Phoenix Park with Thomas Burke, his permanent under-secretary. They were seized by the 'Invincibles', a gang led by Edward McCaffrey, an Irish-American, and butchered with 12-inch surgical knives.

The Irish, it must be said, had a genius for making the worst of a good cause. The Liberal cabinet minister Joseph Chamberlain commented that, had they pursued their aims within the law and without violence, there was 'no agitation in the United Kingdom more deserving of untiring sympathy, and more entitled to complete success'. But they did not do that.

'The more one does for the Irish', the Queen said, 'the more unruly and ungrateful they seem to be.' She had a point. Gladstone saw through a Land Act giving greater security of tenure and fairer rents to Irish tenants. It hurt landlords enough for Lord Lansdowne to resign from the cabinet in protest. But Parnell refused to accept it and urged his followers to withhold their rents. He was arrested and imprisoned in Kilmainham jail for incitement – an excellent favour, for those who had mistrusted him as a Protestant landowner now saw him as a martyr to the cause. A secret accord was reached, and he was soon released.

'Landlordism' was not as rampant as nationalists claimed. And it concealed the fact that Catholics often exploited one another. Labourers, a commission found, were 'oppressed by farmers' who left them 'more wretched than the blacks of Cuba'. One witness in Co Louth said: 'Every class in this country oppresses the class below it, until you come to the most wretched class … There is no exaction practised by their superiors that they do not practice upon those below them.'

Neither were evictions all that common. Around 3 to 4 per cent of tenants suffered the fate over the 25 years to 1880. The slump in farming that began in the 1870s was being felt in English, Scottish and Welsh counties, too. But the level of wretchedness at which the Irish began made the effects harder to bear, and Parnell had transformed nationalism. He turned it from the dream of cattle maimers and arsonists into the focused objective of a disciplined group of 60 Home Rule MPs.

Chamberlain warned Gladstone in 1882 that Irish MPs were acting 'as if their object were to disgust, embitter and prejudice all English opinion'.

MPs for Home Rule

The Home Rule Party was in some respects the most modern political party in the United Kingdom. Parnell ran it with tight discipline and much care went into the selection of candidates. It raised party funds, from which its less prosperous MPs were paid. The Irish MPs did not set out to win friends at Westminster. They used filibustering – making interminable speeches, droning on and on into the early hours – to oppose legislation they did not like. This was an affront to the spirit if not to the rules of Parliament. When Gladstone pledged that the government would carry its Coercion Bill for Ireland at that sitting, Irish MPs were still on

continued on page 38

EVICTIONS AND THE DISPOSSESSED

Tenant farmers – and the great bulk of Irish farm land was owned by landlords who rented it out to tenants – were often in desperate straits in the 1880s. Blight brought failures of the potato crop, while the cheap price of imported American corn drove down the value of the limited crop of harvestable potatoes. Evictions for non-payment of rent grew as the decade progressed, with a battering ram often the

brutal means of breaking into the tenant's home. The photograph below captured a battering ram in operation in 1888 on the estate of Captain Hector Vandeleur in County Clare. The huge tripod was erected by his bailiff, while the tenant has blocked up the windows with earth and branches.

The photographer also recorded another family evicted by Captain Vandeleur (below right). The old man in the centre is Pat

Specelly, with his women folk and children around him. A policeman can be seen over Specelly's shoulder, making sure that this ruination of a family does not lead to a breach of the peace. A similar fate befell this tenant of a smallholding in County Donegal (top right). The family's few sticks of furniture have been removed outside. The bailiff was quite indifferent to the plight of a young wife and children.

PATT SELLEGY & FAMILY AFTER BEING EVICTED (VADELPHI ESTATE)

their feet 41 hours later. The Speaker closed the debate by taking a vote, an unprecedented action. 'Never was there such a state of things', the Queen wrote, complaining that nothing better could be expected from MPs 'of such a low and revolutionary kind'. A guillotine was later officially introduced.

Chamberlain warned Gladstone in 1882 that the Irish MPs were acting 'as if their object were to disgust, embitter and prejudice all English opinion'. Indeed, so well had they done this already that it would be simple to whip up anti-Irish riots in every large town 'almost as formidable as the anti-Jewish pogroms in Russia'.

Bombings and political upsets

The Irish Secretary W E Fowler survived on 22 April, 1882, only because he caught an earlier train than the one his would-be murderers were waiting on. His successor, Lord Frederick Cavendish, was less fortunate in Phoenix Park. Indiscriminate bombings in public places by Fenians followed, producing mounting outrage. An unexploded bomb was found in the Mansion House in London, shortly before the Lord Mayor's banquet. Hundreds of rifles and revolvers, and 80,000 rounds of ammunition, were found in a Clerkenwell stable. Fenian bombs exploded in Glasgow and Leeds in 1883.

And so it went on. Four London railway stations and the new Underground were closed at various times in 1884 for fear of fresh bombs. Three Fenians were killed when their bomb exploded prematurely at London Bridge in December 1884. A month later, there were simultaneous explosions at the Tower of London, Westminster Hall and the House of Commons. An Irish Special Branch of the CID was formed. Gladstone complained that he could not get a breath of fresh air without being followed by a plain-clothes policeman.

Weakened by internal feuding on granting greater local government to Ireland, the government lost a vote amending the budget in June 1885. Gladstone resigned and Lord Salisbury formed a minority Conservative government. A general election was held in the late autumn. It was a long-drawn out but thrilling affair. The first constituencies to vote did so on November 24, with the last not until December 18, and the hustings were bright with flags and fireworks. Parnell urged his supporters in Britain to vote Conservative. The Tories were not yet implacably anti-nationalist, and Parnell thought they would find it easier to get Home Rule legislation through the House of Lords than the Liberals.

The Liberals won 334 seats to the Conservatives 250 and it seemed that Gladstone had a clear-cut victory. But Parnell's Home Rulers won every seat in Ireland outside Ulster and Dublin University. Their tally of 86 seats gave them the balance of power, and Parnell chose to support a new Conservative minority government under the Marquess of Salisbury. But the alliance disturbed pro-Union Tories. Parnell withdrew his support and Gladstone returned as Prime Minister.

Gladstone shocks his Party

The Liberals, though, were about to splinter. Shortly before Christmas 1885, Gladstone's son Herbert, who was also his private secretary, told the Leeds *Mercury* that his father had been converted to Home Rule. The leak was called the 'Hawarden kite', after Gladstone's country house in Flintshire. It was a stunning development that shocked Liberals from top to bottom, from the old Whig aristocracy to newly enfranchised working men. Gladstone was attacked for leaking his decision to back Home Rule through a newspaper after the election

FOOD FOR CONTROVERSY
Two young Irish girls, Rose McGinley and Grace McGee, outside their home in 1888 (right). The girls gave some food to an old man who had been evicted for not paying his rent. Their charity might naturally be seen as a simple act of kindness, but at the time they fell foul of the law. Such actions were condemned as inciting illegal rent strikes against landlords.

MITCHELSTOWN MAN
John Dillon was the much imprisoned Nationalist MP for Co Tipperary and then East Mayo. He trained as a surgeon but quit medicine as a committed supporter of Charles Parnell. His hardline speeches in the Commons were protected by parliamentary privilege, but when he repeated them in Ireland, he was liable to arrest. In September 1887, his colleague William O'Brien was charged with inciting tenants against landlords. Dillon denounced this in a speech to a large crowd at Mitchelstown in Co Cork. Police opened fire when scuffles broke out, killing one and injuring several in the crowd. 'Remember Mitchelstown!' became a nationalist slogan.

was over. Florence Nightingale said that she had known nothing as divisive for 50 years. The rifts between friends and within families sometimes took years to heal. Chamberlain warned that it might destroy the party altogether.

If the party was to split, Gladstone said, 'let it split decently, honourably, and for a cause'. He did not believe that Ireland could be kept in the Union by coercion for ever. Devolution had worked in Norway and Finland. It was working in Canada. His proposals were moderate. An Irish legislature was set up with an executive reporting to it, but a raft of 'imperial' measures – defence, foreign affairs, the post office, customs and excise, and more – were to be excluded from its jurisdiction. The powers of the Irish parliament, in short, would fall well short of the Canadian. With a fair wind, it seemed, Home Rule was about to salve one of Europe's longest running grievances.

Ulster and Unionists say 'No'

But Gladstone had miscalculated over Ulster. The Protestant majority there was utterly opposed to Home Rule, and powerful Conservatives were eager to do business with them. Lord Randolph Churchill had already decided that if 'the GOM' went for Home Rule, the 'Orange card would be the one to play. Please God it may turn out the ace of trumps and not the two.' A Loyalist Anti-Repeal Union was set up. Popular Orangeism allied with the conservative gentry. Churchill supplied a slogan – 'Ulster will fight, Ulster will be right'. A new nightmare loomed: Orange violence and civil war.

The Liberals turned on one another. It was predictable that Whig grandees would be unable to stomach Home Rule. They included Lord Hartington, the party leader in the Lords and brother of the murdered Lord Frederick Cavendish. Hartington was a heavyweight whom the Queen would have preferred to Gladstone as Prime Minister. He did much to encourage Liberal Unionists.

The radicals seemed natural supporters. Their leading light was Joseph Chamberlain, who had a seat in the cabinet as president of the Board of Trade. He had produced an 'unauthorised programme' that proposed free primary schools, the vote for all men over 21, graduated income and property taxes, regulation of slum landlords, pay for MPs, reform of the House of Lords, the disestablishment of the Church of England, and land redistribution – 'three acres and a cow' – to labourers. He wanted increased state intervention 'on behalf of the weak against the strong, labour against capital, want and suffering against luxury and ease'. This was a man who made landowners shiver – 'I ask what ransom will property pay for the security which it enjoys?' – and who had famously attacked the Conservative Lord Salisbury as the 'spokesman of a class who toil not neither do they spin'. Yet Chamberlain was concerned at the Catholic element in Irish nationalism and was totally opposed to any break-up of the Union. He compared Ireland with the South in the American Civil War.

Tensions grew. Anti-Gladstone Liberals joined with Conservatives at a big meeting at the Haymarket in London, redolent with 'great cheers for the Union and God Save the Queen'. Gladstone introduced his Bill in Parliament on 8 April, 1886. He needed a police escort to get him through the crowds thronging Downing Street and Palace Yard. The galleries in the Commons were packed out. The second reading debate was held on the night of 7 June. A howl of triumph went up when the 'Noes' recorded the 336th MP to enter their lobby. They had won. Home Rule was thrown out by 341 votes to 311.

LIBERAL UNIONIST

Joseph Chamberlain was a man of many parts. He made a fortune from manufacturing nuts and bolts, before becoming a splendid, radical, slum-clearing mayor of his native Birmingham. He remained an unashamed local patriot – the reformer Beatrice Webb said of him that he believed 'Birmingham society is superior in earnestness, sincerity and natural intelligence to any society in the United Kingdom'. But as a Liberal Cabinet minister, Chamberlain was implacably opposed to Home Rule for Ireland. 'I believe that anti-Irish feeling is very strong with our best friends', he said in January 1886, 'the respectable artisans and the non-conformists.' He was prepared to split the Liberal Party to maintain the Union.

A new election and a new force

This precipitated a fresh general election in July 1886. Most of the Whig peerage, and many Liberal intellectuals and businessmen, moved over to the Conservatives. Those who could not go that far joined Chamberlain as Liberal Unionists.

In Ireland itself, Parnell underestimated the ruthless, non-stop hostility of the Ulster Protestants. Irish nationalism had a romantic side to it: sad songs, martyrdom, a Gaelic identity and ethnicity that flourished with the new growth of Gaelic games – the Gaelic Athletic Association was founded in 1884. But the Unionists of Ulster had their symbols and heroes, too: fifes and drums, orange sashes, marches, memories of the Apprentice Boys and the battle of the Boyne. As Irish conservatism morphed into Ulster-based Unionism, the nationalists were faced by an implacable foe. The newspapers over the election period had reports that the Orangemen were preparing to arm themselves. Edward Saunderson, the first leader of Ulster Unionist MPs, had already begun to exhort his supporters to arm, and to drill in uniform.

The Conservatives did not win an overall majority at the election, though Unionism did. The Conservatives had 317 seats, against 191 Gladstone Liberals and 85 Irish Nationalists. With the support of the 77 Liberal Unionists, the Conservatives were able to form a government under Lord Salisbury.

Salisbury takes a lead

Some aristocrats might deserve Chamberlain's jibe, that they 'toiled not', but it was untrue of Salisbury. For more than eleven years he was both Prime Minister and Foreign Minister, working so late each night that his daughter thought him 'close to the physical breaking point'. He prided himself on being able to walk from Downing Street to King's Cross in 17 minutes, risking the dangers of London's swirl of horse-drawn traffic as he did so. It was his one relaxation from work; his daughter thought it 'his outlet for the sporting instinct'. He was profoundly conservative, and anti-radical. Fear of revolution was bred in the bone: part of his library at Hatfield House, his ultra-stately home, was devoted to French newspapers and pamphlets from the time of the Revolution.

Salisbury avoided confrontation where he could – his concept of perfect diplomacy was one 'whose victories come without observation' – but he was wholly committed to the Union. The integrity of the realm must be preserved: pander to the Irish and the Empire itself would come unglued. The Liberals who stayed loyal to Gladstone did so with equal imperial conviction: fail to satisfy the Irish, they said, and the grievances would undermine both mainland and Empire.

Parnell was tied to his alliance with Gladstone, and had little freedom of manoeuvre. He lived with his long-term mistress, Kitty O'Shea, at Eltham in southeast London, remote from the revived Land War – the 'Plan of Campaign' – launched in Ireland in 1886 by his juniors, William O'Brien and John Dillon.

They were faced by Arthur Balfour, Lord Salisbury's bright nephew, who became Irish secretary in March 1887. The Plan of Campaign called on all Irish tenants to group together and deal with landlords as a single body. Balfour was anxious to smash it, and make a name for himself. He did so. The Irish were soon calling him 'Bloody Balfour'. He brought in a repressive new Crimes Act. Harsher punishments of six months hard labour came in for boycotting, flouting evictions and intimidating tenants. Suspects could be held and interrogated on suspicion of conspiring to act before any deed was done.

HARD HITTER
Arthur Balfour (above) became Irish
secretary in March 1887. He was the
nephew of Lord Salisbury, whom he would
later emulate as a Conservative leader and
Prime Minister. As a young politician in a
hurry, Balfour was anxious to make a name
for himself by smashing the anti-landlord
movement in Ireland. He succeeded: the
Irish were soon calling him 'Bloody Balfour'
for the hardline and repressive policies
pursued under his new Crimes Act.

Salisbury wanted even harsher measures. 'Loot, loot, pure loot', he had written of the motivation of the Land League. Give in to 'land hunger' and there would soon be 'house hunger' or even 'silver plate hunger'. If Britain could not rule Ireland, Salisbury said, 'what right have we to go lecturing the Sultan as to the state of things in Armenia or Macedonia?'

Ironically, Salisbury was a generous landlord, who remitted rents on his 20,000 acres when his tenants were hard-pressed. But his estates were in England. He had little regard for the Irish and what he described as 'the amiable practice to which they were addicted of shooting people to whom they owe money'. And he was pessimistic. 'Is it not just conceivable', he had said wearily, 'that there is no remedy that we can apply to the Irish hatred for ourselves?'

There were differences between the Home Rulers that could be exploited: some wanted a complete break from Britain, others wanted no more than dominion status, some were violent and some were not. The victims of the Phoenix Park murders were at least targeted, but the bombs in London, Glasgow and Manchester were indiscriminate. To the famous 'man on the Clapham omnibus', they succeeded only in typecasting the Irish as repellent terrorists.

A plot against Parnell

It was Parnell who had bound together the different varieties of Irish nationalists, and earned them the support of Gladstone's Liberals. Destroy Parnell, and Home Rule would follow. A conspiracy to do so used *The Times* as a conduit. The newspaper printed 'facsimiles' of letters said to have been written by Parnell excusing the butchery at Phoenix Park. Parnell denounced them as 'felonious and bare-faced forgery', but Home Rule now seemed synonymous with murder.

That suited Salisbury and Balfour as the Crimes Act – the 'Jubilee Coercion Act' to its opponents – went through. It was used at once to prosecute Parnell's lieutenant William O'Brien, who had links to Irish hotheads in Chicago. O'Brien was charged in September 1887 with inciting tenants against landlords and to boycott those who moved to farms where there had been evictions.

John Dillon spoke up in his defence to a crowd of 8,000 at Mitchelstown in Co Cork. Police opened fire when scuffles broke out. One of the crowd was killed, and several wounded. A coroner's jury brought in verdicts of wilful murder against the county inspector and five constables. The convictions were later quashed by the Queen's Bench in Dublin on technical grounds. It showed the lengths that Tory Unionists would go to, their opponents said. 'I have to say again, "Remember Mitchelstown!"' Gladstone told Jubilee crowds that autumn. Posters with the slogan greeted Salisbury on his travels.

A special parliamentary commission looked into the Phoenix Park letters. Parnell also sued *The Times* for running pieces headed 'Parnellism and Crime', claiming £100,000 damages and being awarded £5,000. The letters were found to have been forged by a journalist, Richard Piggot, who confessed to his crime and then fled to Madrid. He killed himself there, before the circumstances of the forgery and any interested parties were made clear. All those on the opposition benches rose to their feet with Gladstone and cheered Parnell for some minutes when he appeared in the Commons for the first time since Piggot was uncovered. Parnell was the hero of the hour. Even the Unionist press complained that the coercive system could not have been made more counter-productive had Dublin Castle, the Irish government acting under pressure from London, wished it.

From triumph to tragedy

The triumph was not too last. Though his long-standing affair with Mrs O'Shea was an open secret, it was not public knowledge. But at Christmas 1889, Kitty's husband Captain William O'Shea, the Nationalist MP for Galway, filed for divorce citing Parnell as co-respondent. Almost a year later, in November 1890, the case was heard. O'Shea clearly lied in claiming that he only knew of his wife's affair with Parnell just before he sued. He had known for ten years that the two were lovers, and that three of her children were Parnell's. Gladstone knew, too: he used Kitty O'Shea as a go-between with the Irish party. It may be that the Salisbury government put Captain O'Shea up to it, as a way of destroying Parnell.

Parnell thought he would emerge from the case 'without a stain on his reputation'. The Irish MPs and the Catholic bishops remained loyal. But the moment when Kitty O'Shea admitted her adultery in court proved a breaking point. Parnell was legally pinned as an adulterer and his support slipped away. His disgrace would soon be followed by his death. It was more than the tragedy of a man, it was a grave setback to two nations. Forty years later, George V said: 'What fools we were not to have accepted Gladstone's Home Rule Bill. The Empire now would not have had the Irish Free State giving us so much trouble and pulling us to pieces.' And 80 years on, the IRA were slipping on the old Fenian mantle in fresh campaigns.

SHOW OF FORCE
Officers of the 25th Regiment of the King's Own Borderers well wrapped up on winter service in Ireland. British rule in Ireland, Joseph Chamberlain said in 1885, was 'founded on the bayonets of 30,000 soldiers encamped permanently as in a hostile country'. Yet he remained a staunch opponent of Irish nationalism. Ironically, the Irish themselves flocked to join the army. Almost one in five regular soldiers in the British Army were Irish. Joining the colours was an alternative to emigration for young men: poverty and unemployment were the chief recruiting sergeants.

FUN AND GAMES

The Victorians were far from the killjoys they are often imagined to be. They were prolific creators of fun, inventing many of the world's favourite pastimes, from bridge and snooker – developed respectively by civil servants in Calcutta and army officers in 'Ooty' (Ootacamund) – to football and tennis. For themselves, they preferred to dress games up in terms of virtue – croquet, for example, was said to teach 'patience, courage and calmness under momentary defeat'. On stage in the 1880s a golden age of musicals was underway, with Gilbert and Sullivan writing hit after hit, and a young Marie Lloyd charming all before her in music hall.

STAR QUALITY Lottie Collins, actress, dancer and singer, curtsies to the camera. She was famous for the song 'Ta Ra Ra Boom De Ay!'

MUSIC FOR THE MASSES

The year 1880 was an *annus mirabilis* of music. The Guildhall School of Music was founded, *Groves's Dictionary* appeared, and Hubert Parry's *Prometheus Unbound* was performed. The number of musicians topped 35,000, a six-fold increase over the past 40 years. Most of these were teachers, and more than half were women. The training grounds for heavyweight music were put in place – in addition to the Guildhall School, the Royal College of Music was founded in 1883 with Swedish-born soprano Jenny Lind as Professor of Singing. The 'Swedish nightingale' gave her final public performance at a charity concert in Malvern that same year.

Composers were not held in very high regard in Britain. Hugo Pierson's father, a royal chaplain, was shocked that his son wanted to be a composer: musicians were not gentlemen, he said, and no gentleman would wish to be a musician. The young Edward Elgar was bandmaster on the staff of a lunatic asylum for five years. He married the daughter of a major-general in 1889: his father-in-law looked on him with patronising disdain.

The composer Arthur Sullivan fared rather better. As one of a trio – the other two being playwright William S Gilbert and impresario Richard D'Oyly Carte – he became rich and famous in equal measure (see pages 48-51). It was the comic 'Savoy' operas of Gilbert and Sullivan that were the enduring creations of the age.

Show business was another matter. By the end of the 1880s, there were 200 theatres and 160 music halls in England, and almost a thousand concert-halls, galleries and public halls – all part of 350,000-employee colossus in Victorian Britain. The great majority of these establishments were in London, but the coastal resorts were also rich in theatres, music halls, aquariums and winter gardens. Women entertainers more than held their own with the men, in numbers as well as talent. Their charms were advertised in pin-up photographs.

Brass bands and music halls

The British mass-produced popular music and they loved it. The songwriter Joseph Tabrar, whose greatest hit was 'Daddy Wouldn't Buy Me a Bow-Wow', claimed to have written 17,000 songs in the 30 years from the mid-1860s.

Factories, pits and temperance societies all encouraged their workers or members to support their brass bands and used them to win recruits as well as entertain. Though the bands were most common in the north, the Salvation Army helped to broaden their appeal in the south. Great annual brass band competitions were held at Belle Vue in Manchester. *Brass Band News* was launched in 1881 and prided itself on reporting on more than 200 competitions a year. One firm of music publishers claimed to have 5,000 bands on its books in 1887.

Music hall was big business. The 35 largest London halls played to a combined nightly audience of 45,000. Many of those watching were 'toffs' of the

continued on page 52

MILITARY BAND

Big bands were in the blood of the Victorians. Collieries, foundries, shipyards, textile mills and engineering works had their own highly competitive brass bands, particularly in the North. If they were in Wales, they may have had a male voice choir as well. Salvation Army bands brought the distinctive sound to the South. So did army bands, which played on the bandstands of many municipal parks. This is the band of the 1st Battalion Royal Irish Rifles, stationed at Belfast in 1889. Note the young lads in the foreground. Many young recruits were tempted to join up as drummer boys and buglers.

THE SAVOY OPERAS

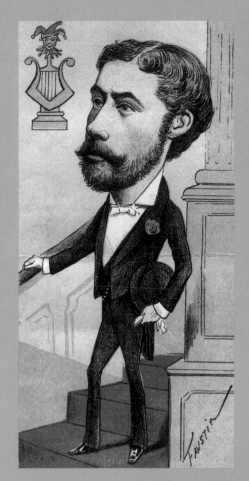

Richard D'Oyly Carte built the Savoy Theatre on the Strand in London in 1881. It was the first theatre ever to be lit by electricity, and D'Oyly Carte intended it as a showcase for the remarkable talents of composer Arthur Sullivan and librettist William S Gilbert. The two wrote 14 comic operas together, many of which – *HMS Pinafore, The Pirates of Penzance, The Mikado, The Gondoliers* – are as much loved today as when they were first performed. With Gilbert's well-observed and witty lyrics matched perfectly by Sullivan's music, they lampooned Victorian Britain and its great institutions with affection, style and not a little cruel insight.

AN INSTITUTION IS BORN
Richard D'Oyly Carte (above) was the impresario behind the comic operas of Gilbert and Sullivan. As the programme cover for *The Mikado* makes clear (right), he was 'Proprietor and Manager' of the Savoy Theatre, which became renowned for their musicals in the 1880s – so much so that they became known as the 'Savoy operas'. *The Mikado* was and still is one of the best-loved of the Gilbert and Sullivan light operas. The endearing and enduring song 'Three little maids from school are we …' was sung by these three Mikado maids in 1885 (left).

HEAVYWEIGHT TALENTS

The composer Arthur Seymour Sullivan (right, 1842–1900) was the son of an army bandmaster. As a boy he was a chorister at the Chapel Royal, then trained at the Royal Academy of Music and at the Leipzig Conservatory. He emerged as a versatile composer who could turn his hand to a variety of musical styles, from classical opera to rousing hymn tunes, 'Onward Christian Soldiers' among them. He was fortunate to find a partner of equal talent in William Schwenck Gilbert (left, 1836–1911).

W S Gilbert's first career inclination had been to the law, but by the time he was called to the bar he was having too much fun penning comic verse. The pair first met in 1870 and began working together the next year. Their first real success came in 1875 with *Trial by Jury*, which brought them to the attention of impresario Richard D'Oyly Carte, who took over the staging of their works. By the time they moved to the Savoy Theatre, they had already produced *HMS Pinafore* and *The Pirates of Penzance*. Success continued throughout the 1880s with a string of 'Savoy Operas' – *Princess Ida* (below) appeared in 1884. *The Gondoliers* (1889) was the last of their collaborations from this prolific period. Both men were knighted for their services to music, Sullivan in 1883 but Gilbert had to wait until 1907.

A respectful operatic perversion of Tennyson's "PRINCESS" in Three Acts.

ENTITLED

PRINCESS IDA

OR CASTLE ADAMANT.

WRITTEN BY
W. S. GILBERT

MUSIC BY
ARTHUR SULLIVAN.

BIGGEST IN THE BUSINESS

Marie Lloyd (left) was a star from the very outset of her music hall career. As a 14-year-old in 1885, she was fourth on the bill at the Star Palace of Varieties in Bermondsey, belting out her trademark song, 'The Boy I Love Sits Up in the Gallery'. Two years later, shortly before this photograph was taken, she was one of a tiny elite in the entertainment world earning £100 a week. A disastrous marriage, to a racecourse tout, did little to slow her down. She was deluged with offers to appear in pantomime, but found it irksome to work to a script. Music hall offered her the freedom to indulge in the bawdy ad-libs at which she excelled. She stood up for a woman's right to stand up to her husband, with her famous song of the wife whose husband fancies a fortnight on his own:

> If that's your blooming game, I intend
> to do the same
> Cos a little of what you fancy does
> yer good.

She was condemned by the likes of Laura Ormiston Chant of the Social Purity Alliance, who made a public protest when Marie sang at the Empire in London – to no avail. Marie Lloyd was a Cockney through and through, the eldest of nine children of an artificial flower-maker and part-time pub waiter, and she gave as good as she got.

NATURAL PERFORMER

Vesta Victoria (above) first appeared on stage as a four-year-old with her father, the 'Upside-Down Comedian', whose specialty was singing while standing on his head. She made her professional debut in 1883 at the age of 10. While still a teenager, she had top billing in British music-halls and American vaudeville: in Victorian days, British stars were much more in demand in the United States than vice-versa. She had fresh-faced good looks and a fine clear voice, which perfectly suited songs that were all innocence on the surface, less so beneath. She had big hits with 'Our lodger's such a nice young man' and 'Daddy wouldn't buy me a bow-wow'. She had a long career, mixing comedy with singing, and her last performance was in the finale of the Royal Variety Show at the London Palladium in 1932.

sort lampooned by the comics on the stage. The music hall season was said to peak on Boat Race night, and Earl Bruce, who married pert beauty Dolly Tester, was one of several aristocrats who proved susceptible to showgirl charms.

It was hard work to be a music hall star. The Scot Arthur Lloyd wrote his own comedy sketches, pantomimes, dialogues and songs, more than a thousand of them, which he sang in a fetching baritone. These included big hits – 'Not for Joe', 'Pretty Lips, Sweeter than Cherry or Plum' and 'I vowed I would never leave her'. He also wrote and staged a four act play, *Bally Voyan*. He doubled up as a theatre manager and music hall proprietor, opening the Shakespeare Music Hall in Glasgow in October 1881, and closing it 14 weeks later, much out of pocket, when it failed to pack in the punters.

A typical year, 1886, saw Arthur Lloyd criss-crossing the land from the London Pavilion to the Wintergarden in Morecambe, via the Glasgow Scotia, the Moss Varieties in Edinburgh, the Folly at Manchester, Aquariums at Scarborough, Brighton and Yarmouth, Pier Pavilion at Hastings, Victoria Hall at Bridlington and Westcliff Saloon at Whitby. His children appeared with him, to spread the load. Though he was a star and the first music hall artiste to appear before royalty, the highest salary he ever got was £15 at the London Pavilion.

A superstar is born

The Americans lapped up British celebrities, be they writers like Oscar Wilde or comic singers like Harold Lloyd, who went down well in New York. His young namesake Marie Lloyd (no relation) proved music hall's true superstar.

Marie Lloyd was born Matilda Wood in the slums of Hoxton, the eldest of nine children. Her father was a waiter at the Royal Eagle in Bethnal Green: 'Up and Down the City Road, In and Out the Eagle', went the East End ditty, 'Pop goes the Weasel'. Marie first appeared there, at the Royal Eagle's Music Hall, as a 14-year-old in 1885. She moved on to the Falstaff Music Hall in Old Street, and at 16 she was touring and making £10 a week.

She was not a classic beauty. Her hair was thin, her teeth prominent, but she sent a wave of emotion washing over her careworn, cynical audiences with her first triumphant song, 'The Boy I Love Sits Up in the Gallery'. Her wit and slyly coarse double entendres saw her take quintessentially English songs of drink and dereliction – 'My Old Man Said Follow the Van', 'Oh, Mr Porter' – and rattle the box office tills from New York to Sydney. She never lost her hard Cockney accent

COMIC GENIUS
Charlie Chaplin described Dan Leno as the greatest comedian since Grimaldi. The portrait above was taken in about 1880, when he was aged 20. Like many Victorian show-business stars, Leno began his career young. At the age of four, he appeared at the Cosmotheca Music Hall in Paddington – an 'Infant Wonder, Contortionist and Posturer'. Instead of going to school, he toured the northern music halls as a clog dancer and won the World Clog Dancing Championship in Leeds in 1880. Leno had comic genius, not for telling jokes but for transforming ordinary characters – henpecked husbands, gossiping dames, shop assistants, race-goers – into figures of fantasy. He topped the bill in music hall, but also starred as the panto dame at Drury Lane every Christmas from 1888. He is seen here (left) as Mother Goose. At his peak, Leno was earning £250 a week and had his own coachman. He performed his 'Huntsman' sketch for the Royal Family at Sandringham: 'My friend said to me, when you come to a ditch, take it. So I took it. Well, I say I took it. I took about a pint and a half.' He died in 1904, aged 43, and was given the biggest funeral for an actor since David Garrick. Thousands watched his cortege on its way to Lambeth Cemetery, Tooting. 'So little and frail a lantern could not long harbour so big a flame.'

or humour. When an audience in Sheffield made it clear it hadn't taken to her, she told them she wasn't fond of them, either, and they could take 'your famous stainless knives and your scissors and shove 'em up your arse'.

The comic Dan Leno started even younger, making his first appearance on stage at four. His breakthrough as an adult performer came at Forester's Music Hall in Mile End in 1885. He was a fine dancer and also sang, but it was as a comic performer that his genius shone. 'The funniest man on Earth', his billing said. Like many great comics, a deep sadness seemed to lie behind his performance. 'Ever seen his eyes?' Marie Lloyd asked. 'The saddest eyes in the whole world. That's why we all laughed at Danny.'

At the theatre

Glamour was brought to the theatre by Lillie Langtry, known as 'the Jersey Lily' after her portrait by Sir John Millais. The devil-may-care daughter of the Dean of

THE WILD WEST COMES TO THE WEST END

At the height of his fame, Buffalo Bill was said to be the most recognisable person on Earth. William Cody (above) earned his nickname by shooting 4,280 buffalo in 18 months under a contract to supply meat to the men building the Kansas Pacific Railroad. He was an authentic figure of the American Wild West at a time when the frontier was being rolled back. He was Chief of Scouts for the Third Cavalry during the Plains Wars against the Indians, and also spent time as a trapper, a gold prospector and a rider for the Pony Express. After all this real-life adventure, he put his experiences on the stage and became world famous for his Wild West show. The star of his cowboys and Indians extravaganza was Annie Oakley (right). She had learned to shoot as a child in Ohio, hunting for food for her impoverished family. At 16 she beat a famous marksman called Frank Butler, and married him before they both joined Buffalo Bill's show. She was a formidable shot – she won all the medals in the photograph. She could hit a small coin thrown in the air at 30 yards, or ash from a cigarette held in her husband's mouth. Annie ensured that many women were in the audience when the show came to England to celebrate the Jubilee in 1887. It was staged in London and Birmingham before going to Salford for five months. It was back again in 1889.

PRINCE'S FAVOURITE

The actress Lillie Langtry (right) in 1880, in a brocaded fur-trimmed outfit that shows off her hourglass figure. She was as socially ambitious as she was beautiful. Soon after her marriage to Edward Langtry, she became the mistress of Prince Edward, the Prince of Wales, later Edward VII, then of Prince Louis of Battenberg, later Mountbatten. After her marriage broke up, she was shunned by society, though Gladstone maintained his friendship with her and the Prince of Wales was supportive. She then set herself up as an actress, making her debut as Kate Hardcastle in *She Stoops to Conquer*. Langtry's ability on stage did not match her looks and energy, but her notoriety as a royal mistress pulled in the crowds on both sides of the Atlantic throughout the 1880s. She also became a hugely successful racehorse owner, twice winning the Cesarewitch.

LEADING LADY

Even the great Shakespearean actress Ellen Terry, seen here (left) as Beatrice in *Much Ado About Nothing* in 1882, began her career as a child. She appeared as Mamilius in *The Winter's Tale* when she was eight. At 16, she was married to the celebrated artist George Watts, who was 30 years her senior. They had separated within a year, but she had met some most eminent Victorians – Browning, Tennyson, Gladstone, Disraeli – and the failure of the marriage compelled her to return to the stage. She blossomed in partnership with the brilliant actor-manager Henry Irving. She played leads in the tragedies, as Desdemona in *Othello* in 1881, Juliet in *Romeo and Juliet* in 1882, Lady Macbeth in 1889, Cordelia in *King Lear* in 1892, but her real distinction was in Shakespearean comedy. Her beauty, with flaxen hair and grey eyes, brought her passionate admirers from the Pre-Raphaelite and Aesthetic movements.

Jersey, she was also the mistress of the Prince of Wales. Theatre-going, though, was growing more respectable. Evening dress was becoming *de rigeur*, and impresarios like the Bancrofts, who leased the Haymarket Theatre in 1880 and rebuilt it, banished the pit and its cheap seats.

The theatre was always commercially risky. The manager had to choose and cast the actors, pick and direct the play – and pay for everything: the lease of the theatre, the actors, the costumes and sets, the orchestra, box office staff and ushers. Those with a shrewd eye for shifting taste and fashion in stage productions did well. The Bancrofts, who retired in the 1880s, amassed £174,000, a small fortune. An established West End actor might make £50 a week, with stars making several times that, but the mass of thespians struggled to get 25 shillings a week.

THE SPORTING WAY

Table tennis is a fine example of the Victorian inventiveness for games. It originated in the 1880s as after-dinner fun, a pastiche of tennis played indoors on the dining room table with a row of books for the net, a rounded champagne cork or ball of string as the ball, and a cigar box lid for a racket. The game was soon popular enough for manufacturers to make purpose-built rackets of parchment on a frame, and novelty balls made of celluloid were found to make ideal balls for 'ping-pong', as it was called.

The Victorians invented sporting clothes, too, including striped jerseys and blazers, cricket caps, coloured football socks, button-down collars, safari jackets, chukka boots and cavalry twill. A subaltern in the Punjab, Harry Lumsden, weary of hot serge trousers, dyed his pyjama bottoms khaki, wore them during the day and created chinos.

Working class players

The decade saw the working class finally make football its own. At first, the game was dominated by Old Boys sides from public school. They had an advantage in height and fitness: the average public schoolboy was 5 inches taller than children from schools in industrial towns. Lord Brabazon remarked in 1886 that even a person of average height who walked through the slums of the East End and South London 'will find himself a head taller than those around him; he will see on all sides pale faces, stunted figures, debilitated forms, narrow chests'.

In 1883, though, the Old Etonians were defeated in extra time in the FA Cup final by Blackburn Olympic, a team of weavers, spinners, factory hands and a dental assistant. Professionals were still barred. Preston North End were thrown out of the Cup in 1884 after beating Upton Park, when the London club complained that Major William Sudell, the Preston manager, was paying his players. Reluctantly, though, the FA accepted the inevitable the following year. Preston's Nick Ross was a famous example of this new species, his teeth 'almost green near the gums', through which he hissed to unnerve the other side.

Blackburn paid their players a total of £615 in the 1885–6 season. It was not a great deal of money, but it bought players good enough to ensure that no amateur side was to win the Cup again. Sudell imported players from Scotland and found them good jobs in Preston, as well as paying them regular appearance money. His side beat Hyde 26–0 in the first round of the 1887–8 Cup, a score that remains a record. But Sudell, a pioneer of the modern manager, was also light-fingered and his career ended with a prison term for embezzling £5,000.

The spread of half-day Saturdays was essential to football's success. The Sabbatarians, fiercely hostile to Sunday sport, had real teeth. In 1886 they had

> At first, the game of football was dominated by Old Boys sides from public school … the average public schoolboy was 5 inches taller than children from industrial towns.

THE EARLY FA CUP

A decade after the first ever FA Cup Final had been played at Kennington Oval in 1872, this Blackburn Rovers side (below) took on the Old Etonians in the 1882 final. The Rovers were beaten 1-0. They blamed their disappointing performance on having watched the Boat Race that morning. Their feet had got cold, they said, and they had missed lunch. The following year, though, Blackburn Olympic established the honour of northern working men by beating the Old Etonians 2-1 in another close encounter. The reign of the amateur ex-public schoolboy in football was over.

Rovers were back in Cup Final action against West Bromwich Albion at the Oval in 1886 (right), a game which ended in a goalless draw. Blackburn came out 2-0

winners in the replay, which was staged at the Baseball Ground in Derby, the first time the Cup Final was settled outside London.

One of the stars of the early game was Henry Cursham (left), who played for Notts County. Between 1878 and 1888, he scored 49 FA Cup goals, and to this day no player has scored more. Six of his goals came in a single game, when Notts County annihilated the Wednesbury Strollers 11 goals to one. Cursham's nearest rival is Ian Rush, who scored his 44th Cup goal in 1998. Cursham won eight caps for the England national team, his first against Wales in 1880. He scored a hat-trick against Ireland in 1884. Nottinghamshire born and bred, in Wilford, he also played first-class cricket as a lower order batsman for the county.

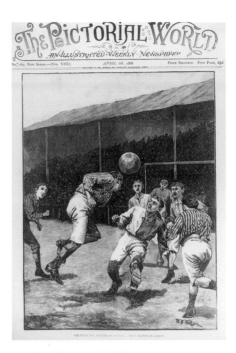

VILLAGE CHAMPIONS

The players of Renton Football Club posed for this photograph in 1888 after beating Cambuslang 6-1 in the final of the Scottish FA Cup. The same year they went on to claim the title of 'Champions of the World', after challenging and beating West Bromwich Albion, the Cup champions south of the border. Renton was a village in West Dunbartonshire, but its club was one of the best in the country. Its winning margin against Cambusland has never been bettered in a Scottish Cup final. The match against West Brom was played in foul weather in front of a crowd of 10,000 at Hampden Park, Glasgow. Renton won convincingly by 4-1. Professionalism was already entering the Scottish game, however, and village teams like Renton were soon unable to compete against big-money city clubs.

2,083 people fined for offences against the Lord's Day Observance Act. The working man's sportless Sunday was established: a visit to the pub, a big lunch, a walk to see friends or relations for tea. The better-off had dinner parties, but not everyone approved. 'Dined at Marlborough House', Gladstone wrote of a Sunday visit to the Prince of Wales. 'They were most kind and pleasant. But it is so unSunday-like and unrestful.'

Saturday afternoon football matches saw crowds commonly reach 10,000 and more. It was good business to own a ground. Bramhall Lane at Sheffield strove for the best of two worlds, with both football and cricket grounds. Football special trains were common on the railways by now and people travelled to see games. A crowd of 17,000 watched the match between West Bromwich Albion and Preston North End in 1888 at the Oval.

In Scotland, football quickly reflected the religious divide. Tensions between Irish immigrants and Scottish natives were steamed off in matches between Catholic Celtic and Protestant Rangers in Glasgow, and between Hibernian and Heart of Midlothian in Edinburgh. Social strains were evident in rugby football, too. It split into two codes, amateur Rugby Union and professional Rugby League in the North. Union held sway in Wales, curiously, perhaps, for it drew its strength there like League from miners and steel workers.

In cricket, the Ashes date from 1882. The Australians toured England that summer. Only one Test match was played, at the Oval. England needed to score

CRICKETING ROYALTY

The moustachioed cricketer Richard Pilling (right) was known as the 'Prince of Wicket-keepers'. His first-class career with Lancashire lasted from 1877 to 1889. He played in eight Test matches, and toured Australia in 1881-2 and 1887-8. His later ill-health was thought to have been caused by sunstroke suffered on his first trip. Pilling's wicket-keeping was neat and dexterous, and he was also a stylish batsman. The public was fond of him. His 1889 Lancashire benefit match raised £1,500, a considerable sum, and the County Cricket Club paid for him to go on a cruise to Australia for his health in the winter of 1890-1. Wisden named him Wicket-keeper of the Year in 1891, but he died the same year.

TEAM CAPTAIN

Rugby Union was flourishing. E T Gurdon (below) captained both Richmond and Middlesex and played 16 games for England during his long career. Middlesex was the strongest county side in the south for much of the decade. In 1887 Gurdon captained them against Lancashire, the champions of the north, for a Charity Festival in London. Though Rugby League was popular in the north, and drew off some of the best players, Lancashire won. After the match, Gurdon was presented to the Prince of Wales who had been among the spectators.

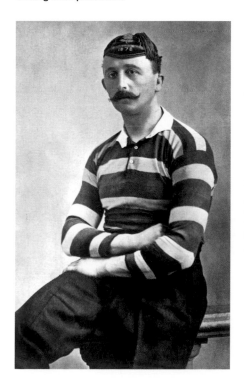

TENNIS COMES OF AGE

Tennis grew at a pace in the 1880s. Tournaments were held across the country, with Eastbourne (above) a particular favourite with the crowds. Note the parasols used by most ladies in the crowd to shade themselves from the sun. Though tennis was fashionable, a tan was not. Even when playing a game, ladies wore hats, full-length skirts and long sleeves – the mutton chop sleeves popular in 1888 gave these ladies (top right) a little more room to manoeuvre.

The first international tennis match took place at Wimbledon in 1883 (bottom right). William and Ernest Renshaw of England beat Clarence M and J S Clark of the United States. The Renshaw twins (centre, far right) transformed tennis techniques and tactics. They were sufficiently well off to be full-time amateur players, spending their winters training at the Hotel Beau Site at Cannes on the French Riviera. Most players either adapted strokes from real tennis,

cutting and spinning the ball heavily, or used flicks of the wrist, as played in rackets. The Renshaws were the first to develop a pure lawn tennis style of playing. They took the ball early, volleying it before it bounced, or played the smash. They were also the first to play in the modern doubles formation: instead of both players standing near the base-line, one twin would stand at the net ready to volley back service returns, while the other stayed deeper.

Willie Renshaw (on the left in the picture) was the more forceful and dashing player of the two. He won the Men's

Singles at Wimbledon seven times – three times against the more graceful but less powerful Ernest (on the right). They are pictured here in 1888, the year that Ernest finally won Wimbledon. The last Wimbledon appearance by a Renshaw was in 1893.

Rev Thomas Hartley (centre, near right) was the only clergyman to win the Singles title at Wimbledon. He won by default in 1879, when the defending champion failed to defend his title. Hartley retained the title in 1880 with a creditable four set victory, but in 1881 William Renshaw blew him away in 37 minutes to take his first title.

In Affectionate Remembrance
OF
ENGLISH CRICKET,
WHICH DIED AT THE OVAL
ON
29th AUGUST, 1882,
Deeply lamented by a large circle of sorrowing
friends and acquaintances.

R. I. P.

*N.B.—The body will be cremated and the
ashes taken to Australia.*

THE BIRTH OF THE ASHES

The mock obituary that appeared in *The Times* to mark the death of English Cricket on 29 August, 1882, when England were defeated by Australia at the Oval. The mourners included Ivo Bligh (near right), who took on the task of captaining England on the subsequent campaign to regain 'the Ashes' in Australia.

England's defeat had fallen on the 40th birthday of Alfred Shaw (far right). With a reputation as the best slow-arm bowler in the country, Shaw was known as the 'Emperor of Bowlers'. But given his advancing age and girth, he had been left out of the England side for the fateful game. He was the youngest of 13 children of a stocking knitter in Nottinghamshire. He worked on a farm as a boy, scaring crows, but was sacked for spending his time playing cricket. He was the most accurate and economical bowler of his time, with a truly remarkable record – more than half of the overs he bowled were maidens. He took 100 wickets in a season on eight occasions. It was Shaw's idea to indicate the batsman's crease with whitewash on the pitch rather than cut into the turf.

85 runs to win in their second innings. They were cruising to victory when the Australian fast bowler Fred Spofforth ripped through the batting and the unthinkable happened. The 'Cornstalks', as *Punch* dubbed the men from 'Kangaroo Land', had won.

The *Sporting Times* ran a mock obituary that ended: 'The body will be cremated and the ashes taken to Australia', and a sporting legend was born. The England captain, Ivo Bligh, later the 8th Earl of Darnley, promised that his side would regain 'the ashes'. He did so in Australia in 1882–3, when England won two of the three Test matches. Bligh was given a small urn containing ashes, probably from bails, which became one of the most famous trophies in sport.

Golf was rapidly gaining momentum as a favourite pastime. In 1880 England had a dozen clubs. That had become 50 seven years later, and soon enough it would top a thousand. Tennis largely displaced croquet, both as a game and as a means for middle class girls to meet eligible young men.

The cost – and the snobberies – of golf and tennis clubs largely excluded working class men. They had their own thriving pastimes. Outsiders were amazed at how miners filled their leisure time in pit villages. They had bowls, pigeons, angling, quoits, handicapped foot races, hare coursing and dog racing, local cricket and football leagues. Allotment owners vied with one another to grow the biggest leeks and the finest roses.

The latest craze – camping

'Camping out', Charles Dickens Junior wrote in 1881, 'is a form of entertainment which has lately come into fashion.' The water meadows by the Thames were a favourite camp site. A party had been seen at Cookham with a servant in livery laying a long table for their dinner. Dickens recommended buying cooking stoves in Wigmore Street, and an iron tripod with a hook to hang a kettle on at Edgington's of Tooley Street. Tents were made by army suppliers, or were easily run up by sailmakers.

Other once-common practices were dying out. Dog fights and ratting matches had become 'as rare as a policeman in the suburbs'. Cruelty to animals was checked by the RSPCA, which broadened out from London in the 1880s to

ANOTHER SIDE TO CRICKET

Cricket was part of the cement of the British Empire. A cricket field was as much a part of a colonial city as the Anglican church, the botanical garden, the barracks and governor's grand residence. The game was well supported in India. This team of Parsees (right), the commercial elite, toured England in 1886. They were not yet as good as they were to become. They won only one of their 28 matches.

Cricket was not an exclusive male preserve. Girls were already playing the game. This beautifully turned-out team (below) played at Royal Holloway College, a women-only college founded by the patent medicine millionaire Thomas Holloway, and opened by Queen Victoria in 1886

become a national group under John Colam, its energetic secretary. The Society had 80 inspectors by 1886, and was bringing several thousand prosecutions a year for cruelty. Bare-knuckle boxing, though also banned, survived with clandestine bouts got up in the top floors of pubs. In fact, most were 'ramps' or swindles, staged to get the door money and bets from punters, then interrupted by fake police raids, after which the organisers 'cut up the plunder'.

Cycling – a new subject for a flutter

The national urge to gamble found a new outlet in bicycle races. Well-wagered matches were arranged between champions for prize money. In one, the well-known cyclist Stanton allowed his challenger, Keen, a half hour start in a 100-mile race for a prize of £50.

LONG-LIVED TRADITION
Wrestling was a popular country sport, particularly in Scotland, the North and the West of England. This picture (right), taken by Henry Mayson in the late Victorian era, shows Cumbrian wrestling, which some claimed went back to the Vikings. The wrestler tries to throw his opponent to the ground, or make him lose his hold. If both fall together, it is a 'dog fall' and the bout is restarted. Matches were the best of three falls. Tournaments were held on Midsummer's Day and at New Year. Wrestling survives with other Lake District sports at the Grasmere Sports and Show, held annually in August since 1852.

Women were as keen on cycling as men, for the unprecedented freedom it gave them. The first safety bicycle was built by John Starley in Coventry in 1885. It remains a standard design, with two wheels of the same size, and a chain-driven rear wheel on a diamond frame. It reduced the risk of a nasty fall from a great height, which was an ever-present danger with a large-wheeled penny farthing. Braking was much improved, too. The addition of a chain guard to keep skirts out of the gears made it much safer for women. The Dunlop pneumatic tyre, in production from 1889, improved the comfort of the ride. The early models of the 'Rover', as Starley called his machine, were expensive at £12 or so, but the price soon dropped with mass production. The company eventually went on to make motorcycles and Rover cars.

Perhaps as many as 400,000 were cycling regularly by 1885. 'It is now by no means unusual', Viscount Bury observed, 'to see, in the neighbourhood of towns, mechanics making their way home from work on their bicycle.' There were nationwide clubs, the Cyclists' Touring Club and the National Cyclists' Union, and several magazines. Tricycles outnumbered bicycles at first, since they were safer, but this soon reversed. As *The Times* noted, 'bicycling will always have the greater charm for the young fellow of nerve'.

CYCLING'S GOLDEN AGE

With roads free of cars, the 1880s were a splendid time for cyclists. Every town and large village had its cycling club. Many people commuted to work by bicycle, and cycled at weekends for pleasure. The big, extensive railway network could transport enthusiasts and their two-wheeled machines deep into the countryside for a day out or for a touring holiday.

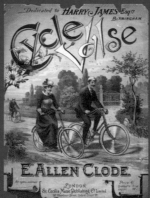

PNEUMATIC TREAT
The romantic boy-and-girl outings celebrated on the sheet music for the 'Cycle Valse' or Waltz (left) were made possible by the invention of the pneumatic tyre. This major step forward in rider comfort was the work of Scotsman John Boyd Dunlop, seen here (below) holding the first bicycle equipped with the more comfortable blow-up tyres. Dunlop was a farmer's son and a vet by profession. He was inspired by the bone-shaking that cyclists endured on solid rubber tyres on the granite-block roads in Belfast, where he had his practice. His patent for the pneumatic tyre was granted in December 1888.

FIRST FAVOURITE
The penny farthing (left) first appeared in 1870 and was still 'King of the Road' when this picture of three neatly kitted club riders was taken in the late 1880s. The machine jolted badly on rough surfaces, though, at a time when most roads were pretty rough. And it was a long way down if the cyclist 'took a header' and fell off.

MYRIAD SHAPES AND SIZES

The bicycle was a perfect subject for Victorian ingenuity. One young couple (top left) are skilfully accommodated with a tandem penny farthing, for an outing at Putney in London at the end of the decade. The 'farthing' wheel – the rear wheel on a single-seat machine – has been moved to the front. Other exotic forms are seen in the advertisement by D Rudge & Co (right), then the world's largest bicycle manufacturer. John Boyd Dunlop's son, also John, is seen here (centre left) on a machine with his father's pneumatic tyres. Dunlop began experimenting with lengths of inflated rubber hose when the boy complained at the jarring he got from the solid tyres on his tricycle. The result was dramatic: not only were the new tyres more comfortable, they also greatly increased speed and manoeuvrability. The penny farthing fought back hard, and, indeed, still has its fans today. Members of the Colchester Cycling Club (above right) lined up by the score for this photograph in 1886. The couple above are posed in a studio in front of a countryside back-drop. The young man in the bowler (bottom left) is astride a more modestly sized penny farthing known as an 'Ariel'. But the safety bicycle, with two equal-sized wheels and a chain-driven rear wheel on a diamond frame, was to sweep all before it. The first one was built by John Starley in Coventry in 1885.

'When the spirits are low, when the day appears dark, when work becomes monotonous, when hope hardly seems worth having, just mount a bicycle and go out for a spin down the road ….'

Arthur Conan Doyle, creator of Sherlock Holmes

URBAN CHILD'S PLAY
Children in towns and cities played on the
street, weather permitting. These children
of mixed ages are passing the time outside
a shop at the foot of the church steps in
Whitby on a fine summer's day in 1880. Of
the more physically active games, King of
the Castle was a firm favourite, as was leap
frog and Blind Man's Bluff.

HORSERACING AND HUNTING

Not all approved of the national passion for sport and games. It grieved the
veteran Chartist Thomas Cooper, who had striven all his life 'to instruct and
elevate' the working man, to find him so obsessed with greyhound racing, pigeon
fancying and horseracing that he had 'ceased to think'.

Racing did seem to be in the nation's blood. The punter's Bible, *The Sporting
Life*, had a circulation of 100,000 by 1881. The sport – or industry – or
horseracing was controlled with draconian powers by the aristocratic stewards
of the Jockey Club at Newmarket. They had the power to disqualify from
recognised race tracks any trainer, jockey or horse that met with their disapproval.
Epsom Derby Day was a public holiday in London. The House of Commons
still adjourned for it.

Keepers and poachers

Some people preferred to watch birds rather than shoot them: the Breydon Society
bought part of the Norfolk Broads and created Britain's first nature reserve in
1888. In general, though, this was a decade furious with huntin', shootin' and
fishin' – and with poaching. The soaring popularity of field sports, particularly
shooting, reflected the urge of well-heeled city folk to gentrify themselves. It
ruffled rural relations. The number of licensed gamekeepers in England and
Scotland soared to reach almost 6,000, with as many again unlicensed.

They were needed. One November night, the Duke of Portland's gamekeepers
at Welbeck surprised 40 poachers, and caught and arrested eleven of them. The
bloody set-tos between poachers and gamekeepers reached the intensity of a
'keepers' war' in Norfolk and Suffolk. These were the leading shooting and
poaching counties, with three or four keepers in most villages, outnumbering the
local police by two or three to one.

Earlier, game was wild-bred and there was no more of it than nature could
sustain. The later Victorians, though, were breeding pheasant and partridge by the
scores of thousand. The shooting estates had game departments, employing small
armies of keepers to raise the birds and protect them, maintaining special coverts
for them to live in. The climax of the season was the *grand battue*, the slaughter,

when the birds were driven towards the guns by beaters, until they were shot and plummeted earthwards in their hundreds or thousands of brace. The passing of each bird was minutely noted in the game record books.

Some poaching gangs were professionals who sold game to the big city markets. Most, though, were simple countrymen out to bring some good food to their family's meagre table. Villagers generally saw them as daring and independent souls, and wished them well. Keepers, in contrast, were not well liked. A Norfolk farmer said they were always 'breaking down fences, leaving gates open, prowling about. They are generally of bad character.'

The Ground Game Act in 1880 eased tensions somewhat by giving tenant farmers the right to take hare and rabbit on their own holdings. This had previously been the landowner's right. But poaching remained an offence – in particular, poaching in gangs by night was a felony, and severely punished. Bitterness over the Game Laws remained in East Anglia and in the other popular game counties – in Hampshire, Herefordshire, Dorset and Shropshire, and in Flintshire, Denbigh and Anglesey in Wales.

The stags and grouse of the North were on moorland and marginal land, mostly distant from the villages, and they provided a living for ghillies and others in remote places. Visitors paid well for the sport – £2,000 a head and more for a week's deer stalking.

RACING STAR
Fred Archer was the greatest jockey the Turf had ever seen. In 1885, the year this photograph was taken, he won the 2000 Guineas, the Oaks, the St Leger and the Derby. His father, William Archer, had been a Grand National winner, and Fred was apprenticed as a jockey at 11. He won the Cesarewitch and 2000 Guineas as a teenager and went on to win 2,748 races, including five Derbies. He rode only Lord Falmouth's horses, a restriction that makes his record all the more remarkable. But his success was overshadowed by personal tragedy. His first child died, then his wife died during the birth of their second child. He took his own life in 1886, aged just 29.

Fox-hunting

Poaching was less of an issue in the foxhunting country of the midland shires – Northampton, Leicester, Nottingham. Here, the Tory MP Henry Chaplin liked to charter a special train after a late-night sitting in the Commons. It would stop at an isolated spot in the Burton country, where his groom and horse awaited him, and he would alight in red coat, booted and spurred. Here, there were fewer keepers and less game, for the pheasant and the fox were incompatible.

As a sport, fox-hunting was not as egalitarian as it is sometimes supposed: the hunting blacksmith was a rarity rather than the rule, but there were plenty of hunting parsons and scores of Leicester farmers who rode with the Quorn. Fox-hunting had kept Parnell in touch with Conservative landowners in Ireland, even as his supporters unleashed the 'land war' against them. As to the non-hunting man, he was, according to Lord Dunsany, 'a fool or an ass … for any man unconnected with the fox lives a little apart.'

GUNS, DOGS AND GAME

Field sports had their heyday in the later Victorian period, as increasing numbers of prosperous city dwellers joined in the shooting in a bid to taste the life of real gentry. North of the border (above), deer stalking was on offer for those who could afford it, as well as grouse shooting and superb salmon fishing. In England, stags were hunted from horseback, not with a rifle and a ghillie. These two gentlemen, though, with their gundog at Keswick in the Lake District, are a far cry from the great shooting estates of Norfolk, where small armies of keepers raised pheasant and partridge to be driven towards the waiting guns by beaters – if the many poachers did not get them first.

TAKING A BREAK

More and more people could afford to go on excursions and holidays. By 1884, Blackpool was absorbing 40,000 excursionists a day, with another 70,000 visitors staying in its hotels and boarding houses at any one time. The more adventurous, and the better heeled, might go to Cornwall or Pembrokeshire. The rich and artistic would go abroad, or to the spa towns and the Lake District.

Like sport, tourism abroad was virtuous and fun. Gladstone thought it one of the 'harmonizing contrivances of the age'. 'The system founded by Mr Cook', he said in 1887, 'under which numbers of people, and indeed whole classes, have for the first time found easy access to foreign countries, and have acquired some familiarity with them, breeds not contempt but kindness.'

People travelled for many reasons – for the scenery, for the culture, for galleries, museums, classical ruins, the churches. Some went for their health, to change the smoky damp of British cities for the clear air of a Swiss sanatorium, or, like Robert Louis Stevenson in 1882, for resorts like Hyeres on the French Riviera. Others went simply to avoid the British winter. Queen Victoria was a frequent visitor to the south of France, joining the substantial British winter colonies at Menton in 1882.

TIME OUT
A few young people brave a Channel gale (below) as it pounds the sea front at Hastings in 1880. A world away from the modest luxury of the Sussex resort, crowds board pleasure boats at Broomielaw quay in Glasgow in 1885 (bottom right). Glasgow was recovering from a financial crisis that had hit the city seven years earlier. The people could again breathe the self-confidence of the city's great industries – and enjoy the pleasure of a day out. Charities helped some of those who could not afford a holiday. This large group (right) is a Children's Mission outing to Aberystwyth in 1885. The sea was an element in common for all. In an age before aircraft and the Channel Tunnel, the British described themselves as, and to a large extent were, 'the island race'.

HOLIDAY EXCURSIONS

From the aristocratic 'Grand Tours' of a century before, the British had fallen in love with travel – for culture, for scenery, for the weather. The railways had made it easier, bringing foreign travel within the reach of greater numbers. European hotels often had reassuring names, such as the Bristol, or Angleterre.

FATHER AND SON

Thomas Cook, the 'Napoleon of Excursions', was still active and not long before had conducted the first organised trip around the world. He hoped to 'pioneer the way for a golden age when nations shall learn war no more' – though critics already blamed him for swamping Europe with 'everything that is low-bred, vulgar and ridiculous'. He is pictured below in 1880. He made his last tour, to the Holy Land, in 1888, but by then his son John, had taken over running the business.

FRENCH ALLURE

A railway poster for Boulogne on the French Channel coast (below right) shows the important role that the railways played in the burgeoning tourist trade. The poster points out that, despite the obstacle of the Channel, the resort is only 3 hours from London as well as from Paris, with 24 trains a day.

LAKES AND MOUNTAINS

At home, away from the busy coastal resorts, scenery was the great attraction, and the Lake District remained a favoured holiday destination of the well-heeled holiday-maker. The Lake District's fame went back to William Wordsworth. Here, a steam ferry on Windermere carries two coaches full of visitors, one of which ran from the Royal Hotel at Bowness to Furness Abbey.

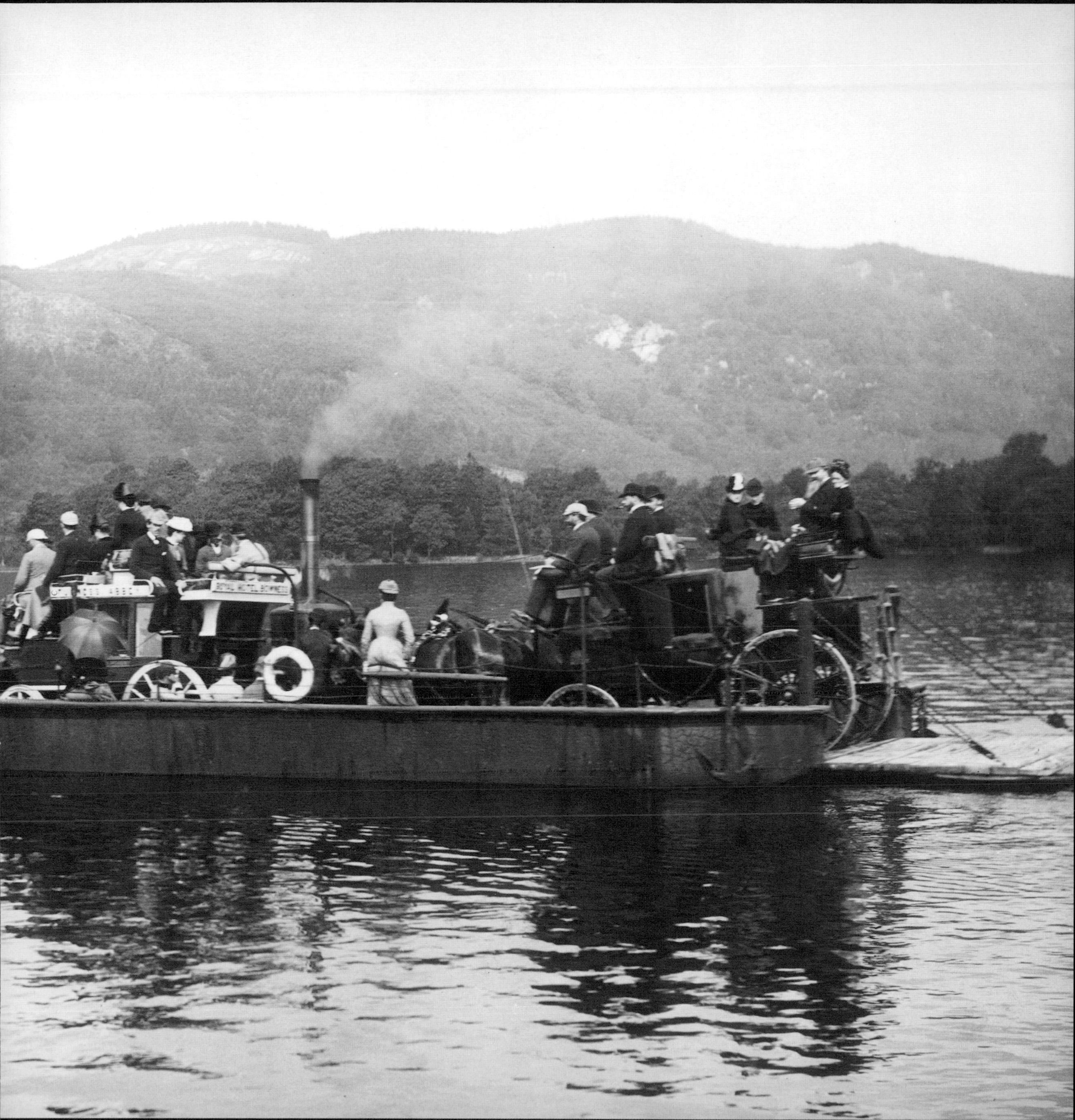

NEW PURSUITS

Adventurous Victorians in the 1880s clambered up the Pyramids, with a bit of help from local guides, and picnicked on the summit of Mount Vesuvius. There was a funicular railway to the top of the volcano overlooking Naples, operated by John Cook, son of Thomas. John Cook also helped to make Egypt a safe and popular destination. He opened a hotel in Luxor, and built and operated luxurious Nile steamers. By the end of the decade, the Cook travel enterprise had 84 offices, 85 agencies, and 2,692 staff, many of them in Egypt. Together, father and son had defined a new industry.

MEDITERRANEAN PROMENADE

A group of Victorian ladies stroll along the seafront at Cannes, the walk of the Croisette, early in the 1880s. The south of France had grown so popular with the British that resorts like Hyeres, where Queen Victoria had stayed, had its own Anglican church and vicar, English hotels, shops and tea rooms. The seafront at Nice was called the Promenade des Anglais in tribute to the English visitors who strolled on it. They went in large numbers, too, to Florence and Rome.

ARTS AND LETTERS

In painting, miniaturists lost their market to photography, in the same way that wood engravers were gradually being ousted by news photographers from magazines and newspapers. But despite the progress of photography, artists remained an elite – and a well-paid one for painters who were in fashion. In literature, meanwhile, increasing levels of literacy fuelled a surge in writing for the young and adventure fiction came into its own.

FINE PAINTER Louise Jopling was the first woman to be admitted to the Royal Society of British Artists. It was at her house one day that Oscar Wilde congratulated Whistler on a witty remark, 'I wish I had said that', and Whistler famously replied, 'You will, Oscar, you will'.

PHOTOGRAPHY MOVES ON

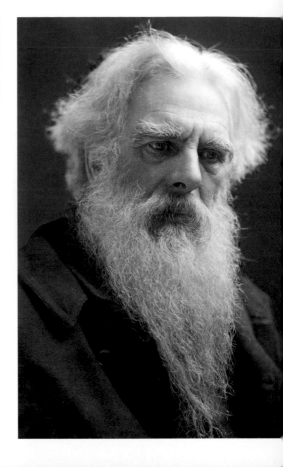

Photography continued to develop apace in the 1880s. The Camera Club was founded in 1885. By 1890 there were at least 176 affiliated clubs for amateur photographers across the country. Cameras were getting smaller and exposure times dropped, so that photographers no longer had to pose their subjects so rigidly. Pictures became more intimate, as it became possible to catch the fleeting moment of a smile or a tear. Henry Taunt was one of the outstanding photographers to use this new naturalness. Development techniques also progressed, although the albumen print, which had been invented in 1850, was still the most common type of photographic print made. The technique involved coating paper with a layer of egg white and salt, followed by a layer of silver nitrate. The 1870s saw the invention of the dry plate by Richard Leach Maddox, an English physician who spent his early working life in Constantinople, and also Alfred Harman's Ilford plate, which improved quality, speed and subtlety and led to much lighter cameras that were more easily carried.

Eadweard Muybridge, born in Kingston upon Thames but resident in California, took advantage of the faster plates to make a 'photographic gun' which could take multiple pictures at speed. He used this to settle the long-running argument of whether a trotting horse has all its feet off the ground at times. He followed this up with photographs of the movements of people and other animals, which he published in 1887 as *Animal Locomotion*. He also invented the first device for displaying moving pictures, the high-speed 'zoopraxiscope'.

Photography and art

'All artists use photographs now', the painter John Millais told Beatrix Potter in 1884. 'Papa has been photographing old Gladstone this morning at Mr Millais!' she wrote of her father Rupert Potter later that year. 'The old person is evidently a great talker if once started … They kept off politics, of course, and talked about photography … Did Papa think that people would ever be photographed in colours?' In fact, Potter's picture of Gladstone was more powerful than the Millais portrait.

Fashionable artists were making more money than at any time before or since. Old Masters were bargains by comparison. Titian's 'Man in a Red Cap' sold for £94 10 shillings. Highland cattle and hunting scenes, or John Linnell's idealised landscapes, made much more. Landseer's 'The Otter Hunt' fetched £5,952. Thomas Sidney Cooper painted cattle and sheep until he was in his nineties and boasted that he could churn out two such paintings 'every morning before breakfast'.

continued on page 90

EADWEARD MUYBRIDGE – MASTER OF MOVEMENT

The pioneer of motion photography, Surrey-born Eadweard Muybridge (left), was a man who had many adventures. In one episode he shot his wife's lover, in another he was badly injured in a Texas stagecoach crash. He was in California for the gold rush when he was commissioned by a wealthy American railroad magnate to produce scientific evidence that a horse could have all four feet off the ground at once. Muybridge had earned a reputation as a brilliant and original photographer. He designed a high speed shutter and speeded up the exposure by recording a silhouette of the galloping horse against a white sheet. The pictures he produced proved that a horse does indeed take all four feet off the ground at a certain point during a gallop. Muybridge continued photographing people and animals in motion: the man doing a headspring below was recorded in about 1884. Muybridge later became the first to demonstrate photographic motion pictures taken from life, with a device he called the zoopraxiscope. It was to lead to modern film-making.

THE PRE-RAPHAELITE CIRCLE

Fashionable Victorian artists became seriously rich men, while many painters now considered 'greats' were ignored. French Impressionists were bargains. A painting by Titian, one of the greatest artists of the Renaissance, went for less than £100. Paintings of livestock by Thomas Sidney Cooper – 'the painter of bucolics', one critic wrote, 'who reigns supreme in the farm-yard' – went for thousands. Cooper was still painting in his 99th year: his funeral was in Canterbury Cathedral, and he left £47,413, then a fortune. A little talent went a long way.

LEADING ARTISTS

The three leading artists of the 'Pre-Raphaelite Brotherhood' were Holman Hunt, Millais and Rossetti. They sought to recreate the simple and direct sincerity of pre-Renaissance painting. Their subjects were often religious, poetic or historical, and executed with bright colour, skilful draughtsmanship and exquisite detail. Millais said they had 'but one idea – to present on canvas what they saw in Nature'. Holman Hunt's 'The Light of the World' (left) is a symbolic picture of Christ. Millais turned his hand to portraiture, with a fine picture of Benjamin Disraeli (below left) painted in 1881 shortly before the former Prime Minister's death. Millais used his grandson as the model for his most famous painting, 'Bubbles' (below) in 1886. It was bought by Pears Soap and mass-reproduced in advertisements.

ARTISTS IN THEIR STUDIOS
Frederick Leighton (above) was best known for his great series of processional paintings, 'Cimabue's Madonna', 'The Syracusan Bride', 'The Daphnephoria' and 'Captive Andromache'. He had the good fortune that the first of these was bought by Queen Victoria. His 'Wedded', painted in 1882, was a mass bestseller as a photogravure reproduction. He became president of the Royal Academy and a peer.

Sir John Everett Millais (left) was unimpressed when told a lawyer could make £20,000 a year. 'I should have made £40,000 had I not given myself a holiday of four months in the year', he said in 1884. He thought it was pretentious nonsense to suppose that true artists starved in garrets.

ROMAN DECADENCE
Lawrence Alma-Tadema (far left) had arrived in England from the Low Countries in 1870 and became hugely popular as an artist. His parents had only allowed him to give up legal studies and paint because he was diagnosed as a consumptive when he was a boy and was not expected to live a long life. He specialised in classic scenes from Greek, Roman and Egyptian antiquity. His later work showed the dark and decadent side of Rome. This is a study (left) for 'The Roses of Heliogabulus' made in 1888. It depicts a mad emperor smothering his dinner guests under a downpour of rose petals.

'The poor Poet, Musician & Painter are the pets of the philanthropic dilettanti.'

Sir John Everett Millais

WORKING PARTNERSHIP
William Morris (far right, seated) was a polymath: artist, designer, writer, publisher, shop owner, leader of the Arts & Craft Movement, and pioneer socialist. He is seen here with his lifelong friend, the painter Edward Burne-Jones. Morris was a man who saw his many enthusiasms through. When he determined to revive hand-weaving, he set up a loom in his bedroom and was up at dawn to take advantage of the best natural light. The 'Alleluia' tapestry (right) was made by Morris to Burne-Jones's design. Morris wished to bring art to working people, but his dazzling success was with the middle class. He complained that 'I spend my life ministering to the swinish luxury of the rich'.

Popular painters

Millais had founded the Pre-Raphaelites with Rossetti and Holman Hunt. He was still active in the 1880s, earning between £20,000 and £40,000 a year, largely from prints. Holman Hunt was also financially successful. He left £163,000 earned from romantic paintings of the Arthurian legends, like the 'Lady of Shallot', which the Victorians loved so well. He slipped up a little with a Biblical scene, 'Finding the Saviour in the Temple'. He sold it to the dealer Ernest Gambart for 5,500 guineas and Gambart span a pretty profit. He hired a display room and exhibited the painting to the paying public at a shilling a head. That brought him £4,000, and gave the painting enough publicity for him to make a further £5,000 from engravings. He then offloaded the painting itself for £1,500. Exhibitions of single paintings were big business. Holman Hunt's 'The Light of the World' was taken on a tour of Australia and New Zealand.

Edward Burne-Jones, simple 'Ned Jones' until he realised the value of glamour, earned a knighthood with his romantic if contrived mannerism. Lawrence Alma-Tadema, another double-barrelled painter, created idyllic classical scenes aimed at collectors as pretentious as himself. He laid so much marble in his house that visitors to his recitals, performed by figures as grand as Caruso, were asked to wear slippers to spare the floors.

William Frith's giant canvasses of Victorian scenes brought him a fine house, sent his sons to school at Harrow, and enabled him to keep a secret parallel establishment for his mistress and their seven children. Frederick Leighton, a doctor's son from Scarborough, painted nostalgic, detailed scenes, like 'Wedded' in 1882. They appealed to the average taste and sold in great numbers in photogravure reproduction to hang on parlour walls. He earned enough to build himself a splendid palatial house in Kensington, which he called Leighton House, and he was eventually given a peerage.

The great rebel against sentimental Victorian subject painting was Whistler. American born, with a boyhood in St Petersburg, Whistler had lived in London since 1863. Ruskin accused him of 'flinging a pot of paint in the public's face'. He sued, won a farthing's damages and published a book, *The Gentle Art of Making Enemies*, in 1890. For him, even portraits were studies in colour and tones. He titled his famous portrait of his mother 'An Arrangement in Grey and Black', while paintings like his 'Battersea Bridge' were Nocturnes.

POETRY AND PROSE
The poet and novelist Thomas Hardy (above, in 1884) was born and bred in a Dorset hamlet, in a cottage built of mud and thatch by his great-grandfather. He was apprenticed as a teenager to a local architect and spent some years in London, but he returned to his native Dorset as soon as circumstances allowed. His novels draw heavily on his love of his native county, and his brilliance shines through in works such as *Far From the Madding Crowd* (1874), *The Mayor of Casterbridge* (1886) and *Tess of the d'Urbervilles* (1891). His love poems are some of the most poignant in the English language.

LITERARY ADVANCES

By the 1880s almost 400 new novels were being published every year, as well as huge numbers of grammars, cookbooks, guides to etiquette and the classics, Bunyan as well as Shakespeare. Disraeli returned to writing in retirement. His novel *Endymion* was published in 1880, along with Tennyson's Ballads and Thomas Hardy's *The Trumpet Major*. The young Irish poet, playwright and wit Oscar Wilde published his first volume of poetry, *Patience*, the following year. He then set off on a lecture tour of the United States, stating on his arrival at customs that he had 'only my genius' to declare.

Another great poet of the age was Gerard Manley Hopkins, though he was quite unknown and unpublished. Until 1884 he was teaching at Stonyhurst, a Catholic boarding school. He was then offered the chair of Greek at University College, Dublin. He had already written 'The Wreck of the Deutschland' and 'Pied Beauty'. He died in 1889, aged 45, and still not a verse had been published.

Much of what got into print was simply workmanlike. James Payn produced 160 books, including four memoirs, 46 novels, eight collections of short stories and 17 books of essays. He thought nine months the minimum needed to turn out a 3-volume novel 'worth reading', and complained that a competent painter could produce three pictures in the same time and earn a great deal more.

The indefatigable Margaret Oliphant was barely 30 when she was widowed, and left with debts of £1,000 and a family to support. She wrote almost a hundred novels – the 'Chronicles of Carlingford' series, *Hester* in 1883, *Lady Car* in 1889 – plus biographies, travel books and books on a favourite Victorian theme: the supernatural.

The world of spiritualism, mediums and psychics was a late-flowering Victorian obsession, and the Society for Psychical Research was founded in 1882. It was a sober and scientifically minded affair. Its founders included W H Myers, poet, classical scholar and schools inspector, and its members were to include two prime ministers, Gladstone and Balfour, a clutch of Fellows of the Royal Society, and the Welsh naturalist and early zoogeographer, Alfred Russel Wallace, whose *Miracles and Modern Spiritualism* appeared in 1881. With characteristic Victorian optimism, they believed that science would be able to determine whether there was any truth in spiritualist claims, or mere hocus-pocus.

WORDS OF AN ANGEL
When Gerard Manley Hopkins (above, in 1880) became a Jesuit at the age of 24, he burnt all his poetry and 'resolved to write no more, as not belonging to my profession ...' But he did write, privately, of ecstasy, pain and natural beauty, while teaching in Jesuit schools. Hopkins died of typhoid in Dublin in 1889, his poems still unpublished. The first edition of his poetry was not published until the end of 1918. The print run was 750 copies, which had still not sold out when a second edition, in 1930, at last began to garner the recognition his genius deserved:

> Glory be to God for dappled things –
> For skies of couple-colour as a
>   brinded cow;
> For rose-moles all in stipple upon
>   trout that swim;
> Fresh-firecoal chestnut-falls;
>   finches' wings;
> Landscape plotted and pieced –
>   fold, fallow, and plough;
> And all trades, their gear and
>   tackle and trim.
>
> (from 'Pied Beauty')

Magazines for the family

Magazines were booming. The *London Magazine* and *Family Herald* sold 750,000 copies a week between them. The great majority of people were literate by now, and skilled workers and their families were avid readers of pages jam-packed with adventure stories and romance, do-it-yourself hints, family advice, cartoons and brain-teasers. Novels were often serialised in magazines like *Cornhill* and *Vanity Fair*. This altered the plot in itself, as each episode had to end on a high note to hold the reader's attention for the next issue. The magazine publishers had writers alter plots and characters to take account of their readers' views. If a particular character caught the readers' attention, the writer would be asked to give him, or her, a larger role in the next instalment.

The new commercial circulating libraries made handsome profits as pioneers of renting out home entertainment. For a guinea a year, subscribers could borrow one volume at a time, and change it as often as they liked. W H Smith were active in the field, but the giant was Mudie's, which had local agents across the country and made great use of the Post Office's nationwide deliveries to post out books to subscribers in the most remote places.

BOY'S OWN ADVENTURE
It was a grand age to be a child who could read – as most now could. *The Boy's Own Paper* first appeared in 1879, and the *Girl's Own* a year later, published by the Religious Tract Society. That did not mean that they were worthy but dull. They were full of tales of derring-do. An early front page of *Boy's Own* (above) covers the true story of Charles Jamrach as he struggles to free an 8-year-old boy from the jaws of a tiger. Jamrach was the biggest dealer in wild animals in the world, with an Emporium close to the London docks, where seafarers brought him animals, which he looked after until they were bought by zoos and naturalists. A newly arrived Bengal tiger escaped and trotted down the road. Everyone scattered, except for a young boy who went up to stroke its nose. It felled him with a swipe of its paw, and was carrying him off down an alley when Jamrach forced it to release him. Neither tiger nor boy – nor Charles Jamrach – was hurt.

Publishing firsts

Two great and long-lasting enterprises began in the 1880s. One was the *Oxford English Dictionary*, the first fascicle of which – from A to Ant – was published in 1884. It cost 12 shillings and sixpence and sold 4,000 copies. The complete work finally appeared, in 13 volumes, in 1933. By then it was a world bestseller.

The other great undertaking was the *Dictionary of National Biography* (DNB), which covered the lives of the nation's historic men and women in scholarly detail. The first volume, in 1885, covered the field from Abbadaire to Anne. It finished 15 years and 63 volumes later with Wordsworth to Zuylesteinr. The DNB was published by George Murray Smith, a man of prodigious energy and drive. His father came from a family of small Scottish farmers, but went to London to seek his fortune and began a stationery and publishing business. Young George was a rebellious boy, ever fighting. He was expelled from school; the headmaster suggested that he be sent to sea. He was apprenticed to learn the stationery trade, from quill-making to book-binding, working from 7.30am to 8pm. After his father's death, Smith found that his father's old partner had been defrauding him. The man went to India and killed himself. 'It was only by limiting my expenditure within the narrowest possible limits, and by working like a slave,' said Smith, 'that I could pull the business through.'

Another part of Smith's business was as an agent and shipper to the colonies, supplying everything from scientific instruments to revolvers and newspapers. Smith had started two weekly newspapers – *The Overland Mail*, with British news for readers in the colonies, and *The Homeward Mail*, with imperial news for readers at home. The Indian Mutiny almost ruined him: 'Our customers were mainly men in the army. We supplied them with pistols, saddles, provisions, books, equipment of every kind. But in the Mutiny so many of our debtors were killed that a large amount was lost to us.' In good Scots style, his sentiment was more with the lost money than with the unfortunate debtors.

As a publisher, Smith swept up the Brontës, George Eliot, the Brownings and Trollope. His titles ran from *Jane Eyre* to *Notes on Shoeing Horses*. He founded the *Cornhill* magazine, edited by Thackeray, and the influential *Pall Mall Gazette*. He thrived on hard work and had a bedroom fitted up near his Pall Mall office, where he would sleep, bathe and have breakfast, darting home to Hampstead only for dinner. The DNB was a prodigious work for an individual to finance, but Smith's business genius had given him funds equal to the task. The work now covers 55,000 lives. Aside from his newspapers, books and colonial agents, he bought the Apollinaris company in 1880 to import German mineral water. Apollinaris was on every fashionable table across the land. Smith made £30,000 profit a year before selling his shares in 1897 for £600,000. He left £931,968 13 shillings and 4 pence on his death, one of the great fortunes of the age.

Children's literacy

A new publishing phenomenon was launched on the back of child literacy. The first children's comic, *Jack and Jill*, appeared in 1885, with *Comic Cuts* in 1890 establishing the new genre. *The Boy's Own Paper* and *Girl's Own*, started by the Religious Tract Society, were patriotic and encouraged healthy, educational pursuits like bird spotting. They ran serialised schools stories, with scientific and sports pages, and photographic competitions. *The Boy's Own* raised enough money to buy two lifeboats.

Such developments reflected a young and literate people. A quarter of the population of England and Wales in the 1881 census were under 10, and 46 per cent were under 20. The churches had much to do with education and the wholesome entertainment of children. In 1887, more than 2 million children were attending Anglican Sunday schools, and 3 million more went to those of other denominations. These figures were exceptionally high – the 1881 census recorded a total of only 6.6 million children between the ages of five and 14 – and the impact on literacy was huge.

At the same time, child abuse was tackled. The National Society for the Prevention of Cruelty to Children became a national organisation in 1889: the RSCPA predated the NSPCC by 65 years, evidence perhaps that the British were more sentimental about animals than children. The NSPCC's 'Children's Charter' of the same year made it easier for courts to get evidence of cruelty within the family and introduced new penalties for it, and fresh restrictions on child labour.

The numbers on the registers of inspected elementary schools in England and Wales rocketed from 1,152,000 in 1870 to 4,688,000 by 1888. Elementary education was made compulsory in 1880. These inspected schools were small, with an average of 244 pupils, which made them expensive but efficient and well-disciplined. By 1888, attendance levels had reached 77 per cent of all children, despite the desire by many parents for their children to be earning a much-needed

KINDNESS TO ANIMALS

Cruelty to farm animals was the original inspiration for the foundation, in 1824, of the Royal Society for the Prevention of Cruelty to Animals (RSPCA), the first animal welfare charity in the world. Among its sponsors was William Wilberforce, famous for his work to abolish slavery. At first, the RSPCA was run by volunteers, who inspected markets and slaughterhouses and brought suspected offenders to court, but they were soon supplemented by paid Inspectors. Here, an RSPCA Inspector checks the condition of a working horse at the North Market in Liverpool in 1880.

Horses were much in the public eye following the publication of *Black Beauty* by Anna Sewell in 1877. Sewell's classic tale, her only novel, told the life story of a fine black horse and his treatment by humans, some cruel, some kind. It was an instant best-seller and did a great deal to improve the treatment of working horses.

wage. Schools attendance officers were tough and no-nonsense men, often ex-army or police, whom the reformer Charles Booth found were great experts on conditions in the slums. Booth saw a virtuous circle at work in the new board schools that civilised both parents and children. 'When children who have themselves been to school become parents', he said, 'they are ready to uphold the system, and support the authority of the teachers.'

There were worries at the other end of the social spectrum, though, in the public schools whose products filled most of the country's top jobs. Classics still dominated their teaching. Two thirds of the staff at Eton taught them, with only a third left to cover maths, the sciences and modern languages. Scientists were well aware of their second-class status. Charles Darwin died in 1882 without forgiving his old Shrewsbury headmaster, Dr Butler, for ridiculing him for wasting his time on chemistry. Darwin found public school education to have no merit whatever: 'No maths or modern languages, not any habits of observation or reasoning.'

The royal commission that reported on the Depression in Trade and Industry in 1886 was deeply concerned by its findings. 'Compared with our foreign competitors', it warned, Britain was inferior in modern languages and in technical and commercial subjects. But this was not surprising. Only 18 of the 206 new boys who arrived at Harrow and Rugby in 1880 went on to study science and medicine. Most went into the army, the law and government administration.

TALES OF ADVENTURE

It was a wonderful time to be a boy who loved adventure books. The writers were of such calibre – Robert Louis Stevenson and Rudyard Kipling, for example – that they held adults spellbound, too, but there is a boyish enthusiasm and zest to their writing that reflected a world where a child's imagination could leap with the explorers to the plains of India and the jungles of Africa.

One reason why the stories are so natural is that the times themselves were so stirring. Sir Richard Burton, whose 16-volume translation of *The Arabian Nights* appeared between 1885 and 1888, seemed himself to have stepped off the page of such an adventure. He was fluent in Hindustani, Persian and Arabic. He had completed the hajj, disguised as a Pathan tribesman. He had been on a mission to Dahomey, and had been consul at Fernando Po and at Santos in Brazil. He had

COMPULSORY PUPILS
Children in class at the Chelsea Oratory Infants School in Arthur Street, London. Under the Elementary Education Act of 1880, education became compulsory from the age of 5 to 10. Church schools like this had a huge impact on learning. By 1888, 77 per cent of all children between these ages were attending school. Many parents were tempted to make their children earn a wage, but schools attendance officers were tough on them – and on children who played truant.

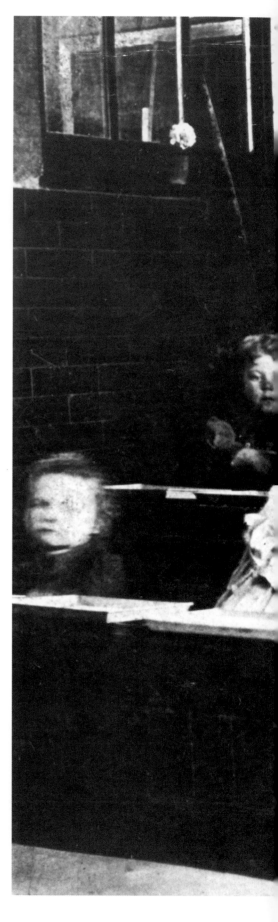

REAL-LIFE ADVENTURERS
The Stevenson household in Vailima, Western Samoa. RLS, the author of *Treasure Island*, *Kidnapped* and *Dr Jekyll and Mr Hyde*, had come to the island in the hope that the climate would be kind to his lungs. Here, he sits on his porch (in centre, with moustache), with his beloved wife Fanny beside him. He continued to weaken despite the Pacific air, and died in 1894.

Richard Burton (right) was an extraordinary linguist, with 30 languages and dialects at his command. He was also a master of disguise who, though an infidel, made the pilgrimage to Mecca. As an explorer, he searched for the source of the Nile. As a diplomat he served in India, Brazil and Syria. As a scholar and writer, he translated *The Arabian Nights*. There was nothing bland about this Victorian.

amassed copious notes, on sociology, anthropology and erotica. Given such larger-than-life exotics in fact, small wonder that fictional characters were so compelling.

Robert Louis Stevenson, 'RLS', was the son and grandson of Scottish lighthouse builders. He thought of becoming an engineer, too, but instead became an advocate. It was a weakness of the lungs that spared him the drudgery of the law, and so gave us his wondrous stories. At first, he travelled widely in France for his health, writing *Travels with a Donkey in the Cevennes*, an early masterpiece of travel writing. In 1883 he finished *Treasure Island*, and followed it with *Kidnapped* and then *The Master of Ballentrae* in 1889. These remain among the most spellbinding children's stories ever written, and they enchant parents, too. While he was writing them, RLS found time in 1886 to dash off *The Strange Case of Dr Jekyll and Mr Hyde*. The spirit of adventure that suffuses his work took him to Samoa in 1889, in the hope that the Pacific climate would improve his health. It did not. In 1894 this kind, courageous man died of tuberculosis, at the age of 44.

A world at their feet

Henry Rider Haggard was the eighth of ten children of a Norfolk squire and barrister. He was chafing as a barrister himself in London when, in 1885, he bet his brother that he could write as good a book as *Treasure Island*. He came up with *King Solomon's Mines*. It made his fortune after a clerk in his publisher's office advised him not to accept the £100 outright fee offered but to hold out instead for a 10 per cent royalty.

The experiences of Haggard and his brother Jack showed the extraordinary potential open to younger sons. Henry's father had thought him 'only fit to be a greengrocer' when he failed to shine at school. He packed him off to Africa at 19 to serve the lieutenant-governor of Natal, a family friend. He observed Zulu, Boer and British struggle for supremacy, hunted big game and worked. At 21, he was master and registrar of the High Court of the Transvaal, though he resigned after an unhappy love affair, and farmed ostrich before returning to Norfolk.

Jack left the family estate in East Anglia at 14 to go to Dartmouth. At 16, he was a midshipman on HMS *Satellite*, supervising the flogging of bluejackets with the cat'o'nine tails. The warship was sent to punish pirates on the Nicobar Islands

MASTER STORYTELLER
In 1885, Henry Rider Haggard (above) bet his brother that he could write a book as good as *Treasure Island*. He dashed off *King Solomon's Mines* in six weeks and followed it with a torrent of vivid, fast-moving adventure stories, most notably *She* and *Allan Quatermain*. Haggard's father had sent him to Natal, aged just 19, to serve the lieutenant-governor there, a family friend. He drank in the adventures that Africa offered, then poured his experiences into his stories, spiced up further with tales from his brother, Jack.

who had preyed on a British brigantine in the Gulf of Bengal. It was thought that a young white girl, perhaps English, had been taken by the pirates. French and English books were found in one village, and European children's petticoats, which suggested the tale might be true, though they found no other evidence. They slaughtered the livestock and burned the villages and Jack took part with gusto. 'It was a splendid blaze', he reported back to England. 'I don't think I ever saw a finer one. I did what I could in the way of plundering. I got some beads and carted coconut shells …'. He was enjoying himself. 'I don't care if we live here for six months as we live like fighting cocks.'

Jack was sent off on an expedition to Abyssinia, whose King Theodore had unwisely included the British consul among 30 Europeans he had imprisoned. Theodore was killed and Magdala, his capital, seized. Jack, still only 17, mounted his own excursion with two shipmates and five borrowed army mules to Senafe, a hundred miles inland. From Africa he sailed to Siam and saw an eclipse – 'the Captain's dog howled and the Captain's cat went nearly mad' – then sailed on for China and Japan. He crossed the Pacific to Esqimault, the Royal Navy base on Vancouver Island. From there, he sailed south to Mexico to protect silver smugglers. The Mexican government had slapped a tax on exports, which the English owner of several silver mines refused to pay. The Royal Navy, in deference to free trade, supported his smuggling efforts. 'A boat's crew and two officers were sent up there', Jack wrote home. It was risky – if caught, they would be sent to the mines as slave labour – but Jack was so bored on ship he was eager to land.

For his stories, Henry drew on both their experiences. The 'white girl' taken by the Nicobar pirates was eventually found to be a six-year-old French Creole, taken when she was two, and her story used in *Allan Quatermain*. The eclipse of the sun appeared in *King Solomon's Mines*, and Jack's Abyssinian adventures inspired Henry's own African safaris.

Indian times and a new detective

G A Henty was another prolific adventure writer. He was a former war correspondent, who had covered both the Crimean War and the Franco-Prussian War. He brought his jaunty, jingoistic prose to a string of heroic and patriotic boys' stories. *With Clive in India*, in 1884, was one of the shelf-full he produced.

Rudyard Kipling had also been a journalist, but his writing was more subtle, his imperial stirrings underpinned by deep affection and insight for India. His father had been the principal of the School of Art in Lahore. Young Kipling returned to India in 1880 to work for the Lahore Civil and Military Gazette. His early books on India, particularly the short stories in *Plain Tales from the Hills*, in 1888, and *Soldiers Three*, the following year, won him a following in England.

Nothing like this for children had existed before. Neither had the modern detective story. Here again the Victorians displayed their unbounded invention. Arthur Conan Doyle created the hyper-observant Sherlock Holmes and his amiable medical friend, Dr John Watson. After studying medicine at Edinburgh, Conan Doyle had worked as an impoverished doctor in Southsea and as an oculist in London. He began writing to make money. His first story was published in Chamber's Journal in 1879. He followed with historical romances, like *Micah Clarke* in 1887. The following year, he wrote *A Study in Scarlet*, the first Sherlock Holmes story in a series so popular that 15 years later the public refused to allow him to kill off his hero and he was compelled to bring him back from the dead.

THE ILLUSTRATOR'S ART

First-rate book illustration, often of children's books, was encouraged by colour lithographic printing, which became technically and commercially feasible for mass production at around this time. Randolph Caldecott (bottom right) was renowned for his Caldecott's Picture Books, like *The Three Jovial Huntsmen* and *Ride a Cock Horse*, and for his illustrations of *Aesop's Fables* in 1883. His style was spare and simple. 'The art of leaving out is a science,' he said. 'The fewer the lines, the less the error committed.' He was also adept at illustrating 'gift books', beautifully bound volumes aimed as much for display as reading. Walter Crane (left) was a lifelong friend of Caldecott. He was best-known for his illustrated edition of Edmund Spenser's *Faerie Queen*, but he also illustrated many children's books. Kate Greenaway (right) wrote and illustrated her own children's books. Her bestselling *Under the Window* was followed in the early 1880s by *The Birthday Book* and *Mother Goose*, a collection of nursery rhymes. Her charming style is seen below in an illustration of children on May Day.

THE SOCIAL PICTURE

Sherlock Holmes' appearance in the pages of literature coincided with the rampages of Jack the Ripper in real life. The 'autumn of terror', as it became known, unfolded in the East End of London in 1888, a series of killings that remain unsolved to this day. But there was also much life to be enjoyed on the streets, which despite social problems were perhaps not so dangerous as newspapers would have their readers believe. All human life was there.

A BREATH OF SEA AIR A trio of young people on an upturned boat, in a photograph by Frank Meadow Sutcliffe taken in about 1880.

THE CITY AND THE EAST END

The grand façade of the Royal Exchange, right in the heart of the City of London. In an era long before traffic controls, and with busy horse-drawn traffic, this was a more dangerous place for pedestrians in the 1880s than it is now. The City was the world's financial centre and a place of business, its one-time residents largely replaced by banks, insurance offices and trading exchanges. On its eastern edge it borders the East End, but the two were world's apart. Those born in the East End within the sound of Bow bells had been called 'Cockneys' since at least 1600, when a satire referred to a 'Bowe-bell Cockney'. The East End had grown enormously since then. By late Victorian times it was a teeming mixture of sweatshops, docks, warehouses, fine churches, crumbling slums and elegant Georgian terraces.

Between the end of August and early November 1888, always at night on or close to a weekend, five women were gruesomely murdered in Whitechapel in London's East End. Two were partially dismembered, with enough skill to suggest that the murderer had some knowledge of anatomy. The murders increased in savagery until the final killing, of Mary Jane Kelly, on 9 November. Letters sent to newspapers and Scotland Yard boasted of the crimes. A postcard sent to a news agency was signed 'Jack the Ripper'. The name stuck. All the victims were prostitutes: there were more than a thousand prostitutes and sixty-odd brothels in Whitechapel. All the women had been married and 21 children were left motherless. Theories abounded then, as now, but the murders have never been solved.

Respectable readers, as journalists filed reports from the East End, had a vicarious thrill of danger. A *Daily Mail* reporter, F A Mackensie, described Dorset Street in Spitalfields as 'The Worst Street in London', a place which 'boasts of a murder in every house', where the police walked in pairs, hunger prowled the alleyways and 'the criminals of tomorrow are being bred there today'. So low were its dosshouses, he said, that the 'aristocrats of crime', the forgers and counterfeiters, shunned it. It was left to 'the common thief, the pickpocket, the man who robs with violence, and the unconvicted murderer'.

There was a pride, though, in these mean streets. The outraged locals held a packed meeting at the Britannia Arms in Shepherd Street and denounced Mackensie as 'the champion liar' who lacked 'only the red cloak and the pitchfork' to be the devil incarnate. Four or five hundred stalwarts threatened to break the windows of the *Daily Mail*, but were persuaded to limit themselves to moral outrage at the assault on a street they expressed themselves proud to live in.

CITY LIFE

The suburbs were growing mightily – the population of West Ham, for example, rocketed 14-fold from 19,000 in 1851 to 267,000 in 1881 – but not always profitably for the speculators who built them. New houses, in Tottenham, Peckham, Battersea and Wandsworth, were often left unoccupied for years. The Tube had yet to get into its stride, and it was too far to walk to work in the City, where the population more than halved between 1861 and 1881, as it became the financial centre of the world. It was easier to walk to work from areas much closer in, hence the gross overcrowding of districts like Bethnal Green.

The 'Old Nichol', a patchwork of 30 streets and courts north of Bethnal Green Road, was the most notorious of the slums. Its rotting 18th-century houses, with their workshops, stables, cowsheds and donkeys stalls, were home and workplace to 5,719 people in 1881. Its 'vestry' or local council was thought one of the laziest and most corrupt in the capital. It persistently failed to make landlords repair or meet sanitary requirements – a quarter of infants died within their first year – which made it a goldmine for its owners. They included peers, lawyers, the Church of England and several of Old Nichol's most prominent vestrymen.

continued on page 106

JACK THE RIPPER – VICTIMS AND SUSPECTS

INFAMOUS AND UNSOLVED

Jack the Ripper, the most notorious of serial killers, got his name not from journalists or police, but from a postcard sent to a news agency by someone claiming to be the murderer. He struck in the open, in the streets and alleys of the slum areas of Whitechapel in the East End. The body of Mary Ann Nichols, thought to be his first victim, was found in the gutter in Bucks Row (far right), now Durward Street. He killed five women in the autumn of 1888. His victims were all prostitutes. They included Annie Chapman, Mary Ann Nichols and Elizabeth Stride (left, from top). Their throats were cut, and their bodies were then mutilated. Huge publicity was generated about the crimes: the front page (below) refers to an as yet unidentified body, probably that of Annie Chapman, on 8 September, 1888.

The crimes have never been solved, but there have been many suspects, often on the most bizarre grounds. They include Dr William Gull (top right), a distinguished physician of the day, supposedly as part of a royal and masonic plot. Another suspect was the wealthy cotton broker James Maybrick (middle right). A diary was discovered a century after the murders in which he claimed to be the killer, but it is widely believed to be a hoax. Maybrick died in 1889 and his wife Florence (bottom right) was accused of murdering him with arsenic. Convicted on the flimsiest evidence, she served 14 years in prison.

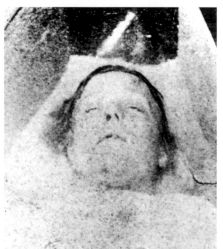

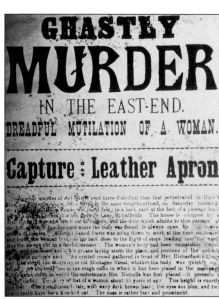

GHASTLY MURDER IN THE EAST-END. DREADFUL MUTILATION OF A WOMAN.

Capture : Leather Apron

'At all times one who strolls through this quarter of town, especially by night, must feel that below his ken are the awful deeps of an ocean teeming with life, but enshrouded in impenetrable mystery.'

The East End described in *Littell's Living Age*, November 1888

BUSINESSMAN AND ACTIVIST
Charles Booth (above) was, like so many Victorians, a man of many parts. He was a Liverpool shipowner, founding the great Booth Steamship Company, and also ran leather factories with his brother. He was an author, an active radical and social reformer, and an early advocate of old-age pensions. In his great work Booth pioneered the modern social survey, producing a huge survey of the poor in London, published in 17 volumes from 1889. He observed conditions for working people at first hand by living with them incognito as a lodger, finding the time outside his business life by reducing his sleeping and eating time, eating a piece of fruit at his desk for his lunch. Beatrice Webb thought him 'the most perfect embodiment of the mid-Victorian time-spirit – the union of faith in the scientific method with the transference of the emotion of self-sacrificing service from God to man.'

Scathing attacks on the standard of housing for the poor were made by George Sims in his books *How the Poor Live* and *Horrible London*. The government, he said, should 'turn its attention to the poor of London'.

Poverty map

One man who did give the subject his attention was Charles Booth. In 1889 he produced a map of London poverty that shaded every street by the class of those who lived there. 'Upper middle and Upper classes' had a yellow tint; 'Middle class, well to do' were brown; 'Fairly comfortable, good ordinary earnings' were light tan. Grey was for 'Mixed, some comfortable, some poor'. Black was reserved for 'Lower class, vicious, semi-criminal'.

Yet the census showed that even in black-shaded streets all but a handful of elderly were employed. In one typical East End street, several families were Jews, the parents born in Poland or Russia, early arrivals in a coming wave of immigrants and almost all tailors, furriers and cap makers. The native Londoners were costermongers, errand boys, servants, charwomen, laundresses, house painters and an ironworks labourer. The younger children were listed as 'scholars', now getting at least primary education.

City streets were alive with commerce and entertainment. Every poor quarter had its market, like Brick Lane, a place of 'flaring gas lights, piles of cheap food, and the urgent cries of the sellers … moveable shooting galleries and patent Aunt Sallies, while some man standing up in a dog cart disposes of racing tips in sealed envelopes to the East End sportsman.'

The eel pie shops were havens of good cheer, the eels displayed on beds of parsley, among cranberry and apple tarts, meat pies and puddings, with mince pies at Christmas. In a blur of movement, the white-aproned proprietor scooped the pies from the oven, cut the pastry round the rim of the pot with a knife, and turned them out onto paper. The night coffee stall was another oasis, its lamps cosily twinkling, the aroma warming the cockles of the heart, and the stomach anticipating 'how richly oleaginous its cake, how piquantly salt its bread and butter, how delicately cut its sandwiches …'. The pie shops had badly dented trade for the street piemen, but their cries of 'penny pies, all 'ot' were still heard in the pubs. They were greeted by the customers with cries of 'mee-yow' and 'bow-wow', though pie meat was cheap enough without resorting to cats and dogs.

In a celebrated study of the London poor, Henry Mayhew had identified eight sub-divisions among the streetsellers. The piemen belonged to the biggest group, who sold eatables and drinkables of almost every description: hot eels

continued on page 109

PUNCH & JUDY PUPPET SHOW

The crowd gives pride of place to children at a Punch & Judy Show in Waterloo Place, London. The mobile booth is covered in bed ticking, the cheapest material available to hide the puppeteer. The Punch & Judy tradition went back a long way. Samuel Pepys recorded watching a similar show in 1662 in Covent Garden, only a few hundred yards away. The English Punch – he had originated in Italy as Pulcinella, first anglicised as Punchinello – was famous for being more brutal with his stick than his more genteel Continental counterparts.

It is unlikely that many in the audience could have afforded to go to the Criterion Restaurant on Piccadilly, which had just been extended in 1880. It still exists, run now by chef Marco Pierre White.

BEACHCOMBING CHILDREN

London was famous for its 'mudlarks' – a happy name for the poorest of children – who searched the river's muddy banks at low tide. But London was far from being the only place to have such youngsters. This group of mudlarks were photographed out on Tate Hill Sands at Whitby, North Yorkshire, by Frank Meadow Sutcliffe in about 1880. They scoured the beach and harbour at low tide, looking for any waste they might be able to sell – bits of old rope, oakum or driftwood, copper nails, scraps of canvas and mooring chains. On the Thames, some mudlarks had tricks to improve their scavenging: they stole onto coal barges, throwing lumps of coal overboard and recovering them at low tide. And for sixpence they would offer to dive into the mud to amuse passing adults, surfacing black from head to toe.

and pickled whelks, soups, hot green peas, baked potatoes, trotters, muffins and Chelsea buns, brandy balls and fried fish. To wash these down, others sold ginger beer, lemonade, hot wine, cow and asses milk, and tea and coffee.

The sellers of stationery and fine art prints also dealt in old books, almanacs, sealing wax, pens and pencils, Valentines, sheet music and photographs. The sellers of chemical items, such as rat poison, matches and corn-salves, included those who dealt in 'crocuses' – quack medicines and bogus cleansers. A typical 'Blood Purifier' was made from sassafras, with burnt sugar and water flavoured with fruit juice, which at least was harmless. Other products could be fatal to the 'crocussers' who made and sold them. One such was a 'silver plating' paste to make cheap articles like brass candlesticks look as if they were silver. The vendor would demonstrate it by rubbing the paste on a farthing, which at once looked like a sixpence. The paste was made of white lead and red ochre, with bichloride of mercury for the silver effect. In time, the mercury got into the crocusser's blood and killed him. 'I have known two finished that way', a vendor said.

Metal articles, razors, pen-knives, key-rings, bird cages, dog collars, tea-trays, competed with china and stone, cups and saucers, jugs, vases, stone fruit and

STREET ACROBATICS

Victorian streets were literally street theatre. Competition between street entertainers was intense – acrobats, fire swallowers, dancing bears and tame camels, card sharps, hurdy-gurdy men and organ grinders, all vied for attention and to earn a living. They were a resourceful and hardy breed. London's wealth attracted performers from far away: street bands from Germany, showmen from Italy, fortune tellers from France. This small group, possibly a family, display strength and balance, if lacking a little in elegance. Some child acrobats were cruelly exploited, though. The octogenarian Lord Shaftesbury was working to protect them when he died in 1885. At the funeral of this greatest of social reformers, thousands showed their respect by standing hatless in pouring rain.

figurines. Women sold haberdashery and fabrics – linen, cotton and shirt-buttons. Curiosities such as shells and bottles of coloured sand were on offer, as were live animals, including dogs, squirrels, birds, goldfish and tortoises. The 'Street-Jews' were a distinct group round Petticoat Lane and Houndsditch, buying and selling secondhand clothes with the monotonous cry, 'Clo! Clo!'.

Curious sights and spectacle

Showmen stood by tents and took money from those who wanted to see the extraordinary humans and animals inside – giants, dwarfs, albinos, horses with six legs, pigs with two heads. Others beckoned the public to look, for a fee, through their 'philosophical instruments' – microscopes, telescopes, kaleidoscopes. There were peep shows, fortune tellers and 'screevers', who drew portraits of celebrities in coloured chalk on the pavement. The thumping brass of English and German street bands mingled with the hurdy-gurdy and the harp, the singers of psalms and ballads, and the 'improvisators' who made up recitals as they went along.

There were games – down the dolly, spin 'em round and thimble-rig. Menders worked on broken china, umbrellas and clocks, repaired chairs, removed grease, cleaned hats and sharpened razors and knives. People sold things they made at home – clothes-pegs, needle cases, clothes horses, workboxes, pails and tea caddies, rush baskets, hat and bonnet boxes. Toymakers demonstrated their Chinese roarers, children's windmills, cardboard carriages, gutta-percha heads, and

DOOR-TO-DOOR DELIVERY
The granite blocks on the house in the background give a clue that this smartly turned-out milk float is doing the rounds of Aberdeen. As the industrial cities grew, there was pressure to build on the open 'commons' where dairy cattle had been able to graze nearby. At the same time, demand for milk was growing. The 'milk train' or 'milk run' was one response, using the railways to bring fresh farm produce into the towns before it spoiled.

CITY OF STONE
The famous market cross at Aberdeen. It was known as the 'Granite City', for the grey granite that had been quarried at Rubislaw quarry for centuries. The terraces of the Houses of Parliament and Waterloo Bridge in London were built of Aberdeen granite. It went out as ballast on ships to far-flung cities of the Empire. Fishing was traditionally important to Aberdeen, but paper-making was the oldest industry in the city. Textiles, foundries and shipbuilding also flourished. In the arts, Gray's School of Art was founded in 1886.

tiny kettles and plates for dolls' houses. Milliners sold their bonnets, nightcaps, cloth caps and silk bonnets and gaiters. Street finders picked up what they came across. The 'hard ups' collected cigar butts, dried them and sold them as tobacco to the very poor. There were 'dredgermen', or coal-finders, and 'bone-grubbers' looking for bones to be ground into bone meal. The embankments that Sir Joseph Bazalgette had built on both sides of the Thames reduced the area of river bed exposed at low tide. But there were still 'mudlarks', children in 'torn garments stiffed up with dirt like boards', who collected whatever had fallen or was dumped into the river – scraps of coal, bits of old iron and rope, copper nails.

There was money to be had in recycling rubbish in the 'dustyards', the great dust-heaps where rubbish was collected. 'Breeze' or cinders were sold to brickmakers. Old bricks and oyster shells went to builders as hard core for roads and buildings. Old boots and shoes were bought for Prussian-blue for paint manufacturers. Women worked in the dustyards, dressed in thick leather aprons and battered black bonnets, filling sieves and shaking them to collect the fine dust to sell to brickmakers – and sometimes finding lost coins and trinkets.

continued on page 118

GOING FISHING

Britain was an industrial colossus. It produced more pig iron in 1880 than Germany, Russia, Belgium and France combined. Twice as much coal was mined as in Germany, eight times as in France. But the country remained faithful to its origins. It was still a nation of seafarers, with almost 20,000 registered sailing ships, more than 5,000 steam merchantmen, and vast numbers of smaller fishing boats.

These pictures of a fisherman and the fishing fleet at Whitby were taken by Frank Meadow Sutcliffe, himself born near Whitby. A Victorian photographer, he said, had to be an 'artist, chemist and mechanical engineer'. He succeeded wonderfully with his studies of the farm labourers and fisher folk of Yorkshire.

SHAPED BY THE SEA
Sutcliffe caught the beauty of fishing boats heading out from Whitby (left), but the days of sail were numbered. The first steam trawlers were already heading out to the rich waters of the Atlantic by the end of the decade. Working conditions for fishermen were getting worse. The fleets were travelling further and staying longer at sea, with service ships coming out to take back the catch and re-provision them.

Although for some, like this fisherman (right), fishing and the sea were in the blood, half of the apprentice lads at Grimsby came from orphanages or other public institutions. It was only by the threat of imprisoning deserters that the shipping industry remained adequately manned, a fact that shocked Joseph Chamberlain at the Board of Trade

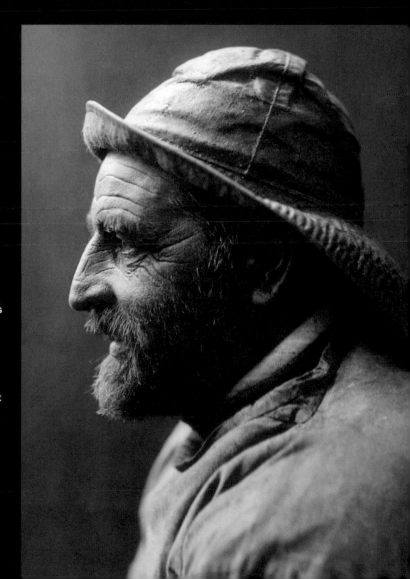

TRADITIONAL WAYS

Coracles were still used for fishing in Wales and elsewhere. These two venerable old men (left) are from Cardigan. They worked as a pair. Each sat in his coracle, paddling with one hand, and holding the net stretched between them. They hauled in on the net when a fish was caught until the two coracles met. Coracles have been used in Britain for at least 2,000 years – the Romans remarked on them – and they survived because they were so well adapted for use in rivers. They float in a few inches of water, cost almost nothing to make, and are light enough to be easily carried on the back.

A group of Scottish fisherwomen (below) travelled down to London to take part in the Great International Fisheries Exhibition in 1883. As well as exhibits, a 13-volume publication covered all aspects of fish and fishing, embracing history, science, gear and equipment, fish stocks and much else. Women did not work on fishing boats – their role was back on land in the fishing ports, gutting and curing the catch. In 1881 Scotland had 14,809 fishing boats, employing 48,121 people, while Ireland had 6,458 boats employing 24,520 men and boys. There were 15,000 boats in England employing 28,000 permanently plus 14,000 seasonally. This did not include inland fishermen like this couple on the Norfolk Broads (above).

SEA-WEED GATHERERS LE HOCQ. JERSEY.

LOBSTER CATCH

Fisher folk with lobster pots (above) in another picture taken by Frank Sutcliffe in North Yorkshire, this time in Robin Hood's Bay. It may look quaint, but this was part of the nation's lifeblood. 'A large number of persons in the British Islands are dependent on fishing for their livelihood', one observer noted, 'a considerable proportion of the food of the inhabitants of these islands consists of fish, and one of the most important trades of the kingdom is the trade in fish.'

SEAWEED SEASON

Fish was not the only product harvested from the sea. This photograph (left) shows seaweed gatherers in Le Hocq on Jersey in the Channel Islands in about 1880. Seaweed was primarily used as a fertiliser, but it had many other uses for food and in the chemicals industry. Iodine and dyestuffs were extracted from it. Laverbread – a food particularly popular in Wales – was made by dipping porphyra edible seaweed in oatmeal and frying it.

SPREADING THE NEWS

The shouted news headline and 'Read all about it!' was the most common street cry. This was a golden age for newspapers. The press was booming. There had been just 14 British newspapers in 1846. That number had rocketed to 158 by 1880, and reached 180 ten years after that. The number of newsagents doubled. *The Times* lost its dominance, in circulation at least. The *Telegraph* was in the lead with 300,000 copies a day in 1888, followed by The *Standard* at 225,000, while *The Times* slid to just 40,000. The Sunday papers were larger still, led by *Lloyd's Weekly Newspaper* with 900,000 copies.

The railways covered the country thoroughly and quickly enough for the London dailies to start to think of themselves as national newspapers. W H Smith organised newspaper trains that left London at 5.15am. The papers were folded and sorted on board. The London dailies reached Birmingham at 7.30, Bristol at 9.00, York at 10.00 and Liverpool by 11.00.

DISTRIBUTION SYSTEM
Hansom cabs wait for fares outside Victoria Station (above). Neatly tended and well-staffed stations, like this one at Carshalton (right), covered the country. The infant railways had become Titans by the 1880s, prodigies of architecture and engineering. They were carrying an average of 676 million passengers a year, up by a half from the previous decade.

Newspapers were both a huge beneficiary of the railway network and an important customer. Newsagents around the country were not only selling local newspapers, but also dailies shipped out from London in the early hours of the morning. The newsboy (top right) still had a role selling papers on the street.

Just as the telegraph gave the London papers the means to gather news stories from abroad, it also enabled provincial papers to carry the latest London news. The great provincial and Scottish papers – the *Manchester Guardian*, the *Intelligencer* and *Mercury* in Leeds, the *Northern Echo*, the new *Liverpool Echo*, first published in 1879 – gave the press real breadth and depth. And they were affordable. The *Echo*, for example, cost a halfpenny a copy, a price it maintained until 1917, and was still newsy enough to print ten editions a day.

The press and politics

It was politically dynamic, too. Parliament was reported on in great detail. Opinion was still moulded by class, party and individual outlook, but it was informed as never before. Lloyd George walked 14 miles to Portmadoc and back to get a London paper with the full report of one of Gladstone's Midlothian speeches in the 1880 election.

As a whole, the press was Liberal-leaning, but the whole spectrum of opinion was covered. The Tory press was outnumbered by about four to three; the *Telegraph* and the *Morning Post* began as Liberal papers in the 1880s, but ended up Conservative. It was not just Joseph Chamberlain who was changed by Gladstone's Irish policy.

Politicians had mixed feelings about journalists. 'These vermin are omnipresent and it is hopeless to attempt to escape their observation', one complained. At one point Gladstone felt himself so battered by the press that he

ACTION MAN
Gladstone with his axe on his Hawarden estate in Flintshire, North Wales. When 1,400 excursionists from the Bolton Liberal Association arrived at the estate, he felled a large ash tree in front of them, gave a speech and led them in singing 'Gently Sighs the Evening Breeze'. Lord Randolph Churchill mocked him as 'the greatest living master of the art of personal political advertisement' – but he, like the Queen, was jealous of the public affection that enabled Gladstone to be Prime Minister four times. He was the People's William, the GOM – Grand Old Man. To the young Beatrix Potter, he was simply 'the Old Man'.

commented 'I hardly know whether I stand on my head or my heels'. But then as now, politicians tried to manipulate the papers. They leaked stories to them, like the famous Hawarden Kite, named for Gladstone's country house, where his son let slip the news that his father had been converted to Irish Home Rule. Gladstone was an adept publicity hound, who kept himself accessible. When groups of worthy people called on him at Hawarden in Flintshire, his country house, they might well be treated to a view of him stripping to his shirt to fell a tree.

Gladstone wrote signed articles for the papers, and he also had a great sense of timing. When Parnell was arrested in the autumn of 1881, Gladstone made sure that a telegram stating this was handed to him while he was in mid-flow in his Guildhall speech, so that he could announce the fate of the man who 'has made himself beyond all others prominent in the attempt to destroy the authority of the law'. He posed happily for photographs. The Queen was complaining in 1884 that she was 'utterly disgusted with his stump oratory – so unworthy of his position'. Another critic was the Tory Lord Randolph Churchill, but Churchill himself was no slouch at self-publicity.

Victims of the press

If the press could help politicians, it could also undo them. Parnell was not alone in being ruined by press coverage of his divorce case. Sir Charles Dilke was another scalp.

It is a fall from grace that most excites readers, and Sir Charles was the perfect victim. He was a coming man, rich, the heir to a publishing fortune, with a good mind, radical and well-liked. He had been the youngest member of Gladstone's cabinet, and was spoken of as the Grand Old Man's natural successor. He had a long way to fall – and, dangerously, he shared the world's high opinion of himself.

In July 1885, Donald Crawford, an Oxford law don, filed for divorce from his much younger wife Virginia, citing Dilke as co-respondent. The case of Crawford v Crawford & Dilke was heard in February 1886. The press could scarcely believe its luck. Virginia Crawford claimed that she had had three-in-a-bed sessions with Dilke and a maid called Fanny Gray. She was also having an affair with a Captain Forster. Dilke denied it all.

PORTRAIT OF A POLITICAL LADY

Lady Randolph Churchill, photographed in 1888. She was one of the most beautiful women of her time, though one admirer famously remarked that she was 'more panther than woman'. She was New York born, inheriting an indomitable spirit from her father, the financier Leonard Jerome, and passing it on to her eldest son Winston (on the right below, with her second son, John, born in 1880).

Jennie Jerome met the young Lord Randolph Churchill, third son of the Duke of Marlborough, at a ball on a ship at Cowes when she was 19. Three days later, she agreed to marry him. They were married at the British Embassy in Paris in 1874. Winston was born the same year. She was a great help to Lord Randolph's career as it soared – he was briefly Conservative chancellor of the exchequer – but it soon burned out as he fell victim to syphilis and was dead at 45. She was renowned for her many affairs. Of her third husband, a man three years younger than Winston, she remarked: 'He has a future and I have a past, so we should be alright.' As a boy Winston adored her, although he later commented that she was very distant as a mother. But she had energy, wit, courage and bounce, and so had he.

RISE AND FALL

Sir Charles Dilke, seen here with his wife Emilia, was expected to succeed Gladstone as a Liberal prime minister. He was an imperialist who was also a radical and republican. He helped to get the reform acts through Parliament in 1884-5, supported the vote for women in municipal elections, and was in favour of trade unions. But his political career was ruined in a moment by a highly publicised divorce case in 1886. He was accused by an Oxford law don, Donald Crawford, of seducing his much younger wife, Victoria, proving that there is such a thing as bad publicity.

The truth is unclear – the judge appeared to believe that, though Mrs Crawford had committed adultery with Dilke, this did not mean that Dilke had done so with her. Rumours swirled. A detective had seen Virginia Crawford calling at Joseph Chamberlain's house in London two days before she confessed her adultery to her husband. Had Chamberlain put her up to it, to ruin a political rival? Was it because Dilke was sympathetic to Home Rule? Virginia Crawford survived to respectable old age: she was generous in bestowing her political favours, too, and took up with the new Labour Party. She never denied or modified her account of the affair with Dilke.

The case was an object lesson for politicians. Half the country might know a man was having an affair – as in the case of Lord Palmerston, who sired several illegitimate children – yet he could safely retain his position provided no word appeared in the papers. Journalists did not buy or publish 'kiss and tell' revelations. But where a case appeared in the divorce courts, the front pages opened and all restraint was let go. The damage to a career was terminal. As Dilke proved, a man could be ruined in a day.

The tatty image of 'Grub Street' was already pinned to journalists, but at their best they included the cream of Victorian writers and thinkers. 'Journalism', the poet and critic Matthew Arnold wrote, 'is literature in a hurry.' George Eliot, writer of some of the finest novels in the language – *Middlemarch*, *Silas Marner*, *The Mill on the Floss* – had been an assistant editor on the *Westminster Review*. Mountaineer-scholar-critic Leslie Stephen, Virginia Woolf's father, was editor of the *Cornhill Magazine* and helped to found the *Pall Mall Gazette*, of which John Morley, twice Irish Secretary, was editor. Walter Bagehot, author of *The English Constitution*, the standard work on the political system, was the editor of *The Economist*.

Several journalists had a distinct Nonconformist edge. Their journalism was radical and moralising. Their hero was W H Russell, whose vivid reports of neglect and waste had shamed the government during the Crimean War. They investigated, exposed and campaigned, often to great effect. Their critics, and their victims, might think them malicious, hypocritical, dirty-minded and self-righteous: at times perhaps they were, but readers flocked to read their often purple prose.

'They are nearer the people. They are the most immediate and most unmistakable exponents of the national mind. Their direct and living contact with the people is the source of their strength. The House of Commons, elected once in six [sic] years, may easily cease to be in touch with the people …'

W T Stead, on the power of commentators and the press

Man with a mission

The doyen of journalists in the 1880s was W T Stead. His background was Nonconformist. His father was a Congregationalist minister in the Northeast, who warned him against the three great evils of amusement: 'Theatre, which was the Devil's Chapel … Cards, the Devil's Prayer Book … and the Novel, which was regarded as a kind of Devil's Bible.' Stead's journalism had an exciting whiff of sulphur to it, as he exposed the sins of the wicked – the Turks in Bulgaria, the coal-mine owners at home – in his brilliant London penny paper, the *Pall Mall Gazette*.

Stead pioneered a 'new journalism', with bold headlines, photographs, special 'extra' editions, opinionated leading articles, campaigns and scoops, including exclusive interviews with Tsar Alexander III and Leo Tolstoy. He gave equal opportunities to women journalists, and employed critics of the quality of Oscar Wilde and George Bernard Shaw. He conceived the idea of the focus group or opinion poll. He suggested that a network of 600 to 1,000 people, spread across the country, could be sounded by editors for their views on any subject. The editor would thus be able to 'interrogate the democracy'. Parliament could be kept constantly in touch with public sentiment between elections. The newspaper, Stead said, would be 'a great secular or civic church and democratic university'. It would, he enthused, be 'the very soul of our national unity'.

The popular press – its genius was Alfred Harmsworth, whose first paper was the weekly *Answers to Correspondents* which appeared in 1888 – dealt in crime, disaster, violent death and the rich and famous. In contrast, Stead's sensationalism was serious and targeted. He published a powerful exposé of slum housing entitled 'The Bitter Cry of Outcast London'. In the 'Truth about the Navy' he claimed the service was under strength, embarrassing the government and leading to a hasty and expensive modernisation programme. Most famously, Stead exposed the scandal of London's child prostitutes in a searing attack, 'The Maiden Tribute of Modern Babylon'. He

NEWSPAPER PIONEER
Journalists and newspaper publishers were the great beneficiaries of Victorian scandals. W T Stead laid into the unfortunate Charles Dilke with the same gusto he put into exposing the extent of child prostitution and white slavery in London. He was briefly imprisoned for his pains, but his shocking revelations forced the government to act.

WORKING FOR GOOD
Josephine Butler (above) and William Bramwell Booth (left, with his wife and three daughters) helped the journalist W T Stead in his campaign to expose the scandal of child prostitution in Britain. Josephine Butler was a formidable social reformer, brave, outspoken and energetic. She nursed sick prostitutes in her house, and toured the Continent as well as Britain in her efforts to make prostitution a matter of public morality, not something conveniently swept under the carpet. William Bramwell Booth, the son of the Salvation Army's founder, was equally fearless in the struggle for reform. He and his army waged war on sweated labour and the abuse of children, and on the brewers who stoked their profits by selling drink to the poor.

revealed, in graphic detail, the entrapment, abduction and sale of underage girls to London brothels. His 'infernal narrative', which ran in instalments for a week in July 1885, shocked respectable readers by revealing a world of pimps, procuresses and brothel keepers, of drugs and secret rooms where gentlemen revelled in 'the cries of an immature child'. His headlines were sensational – 'The Violation of Virgins', 'Strapping Girls Down' – and the references to 'White Slavery' and the sale of girls abroad produced a thrill of repulsion.

The social reformer Josephine Butler and her son Georgie were also active on the issue. They had posed as a brothel keeper and procurer, spending £100 to buy children in high-class brothels. Stead had interviewed brothel keepers, pimps, procurers, prostitutes and prison chaplains. With the help of Josephine Butler and Bramwell Booth of the Salvation Army, Stead bought a 13-year-old called Eliza Armstrong from her alcoholic mother. He paid £5 for the girl and then wrote his story.

Rival newspapers denounced him for 'peddling pornography'. W H Smith & Sons refused to sell the *Gazette* because of the lurid series. Members of the Salvation Army and volunteer newsboys sold it instead. Second-hand copies sold for a shilling, twelve times the cover price, and crowds fought for copies outside the *Gazette* offices. The Home Secretary, Sir William Harcourt, begged Stead to stop publishing, for fear of riots on a national scale. He refused.

Stead was praised by the Catholic Cardinal Manning, the majority of Nonconformist clergy and some Anglican bishops, and by much of the public. Thousands marched to Hyde Park, with wagons full of virgins dressed in white, to demand action by the government. It was forced to raise the age of consent for young girls, from 13 to 16, and to attack white slavery and juvenile prostitution by passing the Criminal Law Amendment Act of 1885. This made brothel-keeping and the procurement of women for prostitution illegal. Unlike previous efforts, this Act was fierce. Prosecutions for brothel-keeping soared, but there were also repercussions. Landlords, now responsible in law if they knowingly let houses for immoral purposes, were reluctant to let rooms to 'suspect' women.

Stead himself was prosecuted for a technical violation in obtaining his Maiden Tribute material: little Eliza had been handed to him without the consent of her father, only of the mother. He served a brief prison term – he later liked to show off his convict's uniform – but his revelations had impressed readers as far away as New York. He later accepted an invitation to speak at an international peace conference there, but he never arrived: he died en route on the *Titanic*.

EMPIRE AND INDUSTRY

One of the demands made by journalist William Stead and others was that General Charles 'Chinese' Gordon be sent to Khartoum to evacuate the Anglo-Egyptian garrisons from the Sudan. This had a less happy outcome than Stead's domestic agenda: it cost Gordon his life and severely damaged Gladstone's standing. The GOM (Grand Old Man), his critics said, had become the MOG – the Murderer Of Gordon. Empire was an inherently risky business, and the advanced technology of steam engines and machine guns did not always compensate for the small numbers of men and the immense distances involved.

A SPOT OF SIGHTSEEING After the invasion of Egypt in 1882, British troops took the opportunity to visit the Pyramids and Sphinx.

IMPERIAL AFFAIRS

T he new decade started badly with a calamitous defeat in Afghanistan. Fear of Russian influence reaching the Indian border, and the refusal of the Afghans to receive a British mission, had led to the Second Afghan War. British and Indian troops occupied much of the country. In July 1880, General George Burrows advanced into Helmand with a force of 2,500 men. He was deserted by troops of the wali of Kandahar. During his retreat, the Afghans attacked him at Maiwand. His men were outnumbered by ten to one, and Rudyard Kipling caught their fear in one of his Barrack-Room Ballads:

> I 'eard the knives be'ind me, but I dursn't face my man,
> Nor I don't know where I went to, 'cause I didn't 'alt to see,
> Til I 'eard a beggar squealin' out for quarter as 'e ran,
> An' I thought I knew the voice an' – it was me!

The British were routed, losing 948 men and 21 officers killed. The Grenadiers suffered almost two-thirds casualties. So did the 66th Regiment, later the Royal Berkshires, whose medical officer served Conan Doyle as a model for Dr Watson. The survivors were bottled up in Kandahar. Honour was restored when General

MILITARY MAN
General Roberts and his staff in Afghanistan in 1880, with the mountains rising behind them. In July that year, a force of 2,500 British advanced into Helmand and was all but annihilated at Maiwand. Roberts avenged the defeat at Kandahar in September. His career was a roll-call of Imperial campaigns. He won the VC in the Indian Mutiny and served in the Abyssinian and Lushai campaigns before his relief of Kandahar. Later, in the Second Boer War, he was to relieve Kimberley and make the advance to Pretoria. He died in 1914 while visiting troops in the field in France. His men loved him, as he loved them. Rudyard Kipling thought that he had in him all that was fine and modest in a British officer:

What 'e does not know o' war,
  Gen'ral Bobs,
You can arsk the shop next door,
  Can't they, Bobs?
Oh, 'e's little but he's wise,
'E's a terror for 'is size,
An 'e-does-not-advertise,
  Do yer, Bobs?

Frederick Roberts marched 314 miles from Kabul to win a decisive victory at Kandahar at the beginning of September. Gladstone's new government rejected the 'forward' policy of operating beyond the Indian frontier, and the war was ended.

African misadventure

The massacre in Afghanistan was followed by another in Africa. The First Boer War arose from the annexation in 1877 of the Transvaal, a republic founded by the Boers, the Dutch-descended Afrikaans-speaking whites who had left the Cape to escape the encroaching British. The Boers saw themselves not as a colonial people, but as whites so implanted in Africa as to call themselves Afrikaners.

The Boers rose in revolt at the end of 1880. The following February, Sir George Pomeroy-Colley, the British governor of Natal, was killed when his relief force of 554 soldiers was attacked by Boers at Majuba Hill. Colley was killed and 266 of his men were killed, wounded or captured. 'Sad Sad news from South Africa', Gladstone wrote in his diary. 'Is it the "Hand of Judgement"?'

A compromise was cobbled together, showing the flimsiness of the British position. The Pretoria Convention in August 1881 recognised the 'independence' of the Transvaal subject to the 'suzerainty' of Britain, a concept so vague that the colonial secretary, the Earl of Kimberley, had to ask a lexicographer what it meant. Hindsight was to call this the First Boer War; a Second, much bloodier, was to come. Gladstone's conscience may have been stirring over the treatment of the Boers, but Queen Victoria was in no doubt who held the moral high ground.

'We the great supporters of all that helps to put down Slavery and anything Tending to crush and oppress the Natives', she said, should not in the Transvaal 'abandon them to the tender mercies' of the Boers.

Egypt – an inadvertent acquisition

At the other end of Africa was Egypt. The British did not set out to acquire it. Quite the reverse. Palmerston had declared in 1859 that Britain should no more want Egypt for herself 'than any rational man with an estate in the north of England and a residence in the South should wish to possess the inns on the Great North Road'. The problem came in Palmerston's postscript. All this rational man should want, he added, was that 'the inns be well kept, always accessible and furnishing him, when he comes, with mutton-chops and post-horses'.

There lay the rub. The inn on the route to India became ill-tempered: the supplies of mutton-chops were threatened. Ismail Pasha, khedive of Egypt, had achieved virtually sovereign powers from his nominal overlord, the Ottoman sultan. In 1879 he was deposed, partly at the instigation of the European powers, and succeeded by his son Tawfiq. Colonel Ahmed Urabi, an army officer, led a rebellion against the khedive and set up a nationalist government. Urabi was hostile to both the French and British, who had already established 'Dual Control' of Egyptian finances. Anti-Western riots broke out in Alexandria in June 1882. Fifty Europeans were killed, six of them British-born.

Gladstone might have preferred to ignore the event, but tempers were up. Britain was deeply involved with Egypt, taking 80 per cent of its exports, mainly cotton, and supplying almost half its imports. A third of Egypt's debt was in the nervous hands of British bondholders. It was too big to ignore. In July, the Royal Navy bombarded Alexandria. In mid-August, the largest British force deployed since the Crimea landed under General Sir Garnet Wolseley. Urabi declared a jihad. On 13 September, 1884, Wolseley smashed his forces at the Battle of Tel-el-Kebir.

Urabi surrendered. Gladstone wanted him hung, as long as it could be done 'without real inclemency'. But the colonel was defended at his court martial by lawyers sent out by British sympathisers, and he was exiled to Ceylon. Here, the governor, Sir Arthur Gordon, himself the son of a former Prime Minister, Lord Aberdeen, gave a public dinner in honour of his distinguished guest. The British were, by and large, good at letting bygones be bygones.

Evelyn Baring, who had arrived in Egypt in 1883 as British agent and consul-general, was soon controlling the civil administration. The British did not formally rule in Egypt, but there was little doubt over who ran it. They often said they were about to leave, but they stayed on and on, in one way or another, until 1956.

The Mahdi and Sudan

In July 1881, far to the south up the Nile, a former slave trader called Mohammed Ahmed declared himself the Mahdi, or Muslim Messiah, 'One who Guides from God'. He had once been in the Egyptian Civil Service and took advantage of the chaos in Egypt to raise revolt in the Sudan, which was nominally part of the

IMPERIALIST TENTACLES
A cartoon of 1882 depicts the British Empire as a giant cephalopod, whose tentacles stretch out across the oceans to claim far-off lands. The tentacle in the bottom left of the picture is about to descend on Egypt. A top-hatted John Bull representing England is at the centre, with Ireland held tight on one side and Heligoland on the other. The North Sea island of Heligoland was about to be exchanged with Germany for Zanzibar.

'Our side in the Commons is very jingo about Egypt … They badly want to kill somebody. They don't know who.'

Sir Charles Dilke, Liberal MP

INVADING EGYPT
The British landings at Ismallia in Egypt in 1882. Although the British did not want to become involved in the Middle East, the slow-motion collapse of the Ottoman Empire sucked them in. Worried that the new nationalist government in Egypt might default on the country's debts, or even worse attempt to take control of the Suez Canal, the British government decided to act in response to anti-Western riots in Alexandria in June 1882. Alexandria was bombarded by the Royal Navy, acting jointly with the French, then troops landed and smashed the Egyptian forces at Tel-el-Kebir.

khedive's dominions. He made his capital at El Obeid. The Mahdi's followers were fiercer and more backward-looking than Urabi's nationalist officers. They detested the West and were outraged that Christians should have any official standing. A punitive expedition to the Sudan was planned under Col William Hicks, a veteran of the Indian Mutiny now in the service of the khedive as Hicks Pasha. He gathered a force of 8,000 men in Khartoum, mainly from the disbanded residue of Urabi's forces, who were sent down to the Sudan in chains. Hicks, well aware of their poor training and morale, wanted to stay in Khartoum to train them. The powers in Cairo would have none of it, and he was ordered to advance. He left Khartoum in September 1883 with a raggle-taggle expedition of 10,000, including camp followers and 13 Europeans. He was ambushed at El Obeid in November. All but 300 of his men were killed. One of his cooks, who survived, said Hicks was the last officer to fall, after emptying his revolver and fighting with his sword. His head was cut off and taken to the Mahdi.

Most of Sudan was now in the Mahdi's hands. The British press, led by William Stead, demanded the evacuation of what was left. Major General Charles Gordon was put forward as the man for the job. He knew the Sudan – he had helped open up the regions of the equatorial Nile, establishing a chain of posts along the river and reconnoitring a vast territory from the Second Cataract of the Nile to the Great Lakes, from the salt waters of the Red Sea to the headwaters of streams that ran down to Lake Chad. He was appointed in January 1884.

Gordon's was a maverick's brilliance. He was strongly principled, a fundamentalist Christian, and difficult to handle. At home, he worked with poor boys in the 'ragged schools'. Abroad, as on operations in China, he sought danger

PROPHET OF SUDAN

A former slave trader and civil servant, Mohammed Ahmed declared himself to be the 'Mahdi', the 'divinely guided one' whom God had chosen to destroy those who defiled Islam. He overthrew Egyptian rule in much of the Sudan, defeating an Egyptian army under Colonel William Hicks. In 1884 Charles 'Chinese' Gordon (right), so called for his brilliant campaigning in China during the Taiping Rebellion, was sent to relieve the Egyptian garrisons in the Sudan. Gordon was no imperialist bigot: he was a mystic, a devout man who had worked with poor boys in 'ragged schools', and he had sympathy with the Sudanese, Mahdists included. He was besieged in Khartoum for 10 months, and was killed two days before a relief force reached the city. The Mahdi set up a new capital at Omdurman, but died a few months later.

and glory, perhaps martyrdom. He was a mystic and severely impractical: as he set off from Charing Cross, he found he had no watch or money. General Wolseley, there to see him off, gave him his watch and all the money from his pockets, while Lord Granville, the Foreign Secretary, bought him his railway ticket.

Before he sailed, Gordon gave an interview to Stead, which was splashed in the *Pall Mall Gazette*. He said that the Sudanese, Mahdists included, were 'a very nice people' who deserved 'sincere compassion and sympathy'. He found the Mahdi himself to 'personify popular discontent' with the barbarities of Turkish rule, which had caused the rebellion. Safety lay in doing something for the people. 'Reduce their rent, rescue them from the usurers', he pleaded, 'weed out nine-tenths of the European employees.' If that were done, he said, 'I see no reason why the last British soldier should not be withdrawn in six months time.' But he did add that it was folly for the government to talk of evacuating Khartoum. 'Even if we were bound to do so we should have said nothing about it ... The moment it is known that we have given up the game every man will go over to the Mahdi. All men worship the rising sun.' If that happened, he added prophetically, it would make it difficult 'or indeed impossible to withdraw our garrison'.

Gordon arrived in Khartoum in February 1884. The siege began on 18 March. Gordon refused to evacuate, as ordered. Instead, he set about administering the city, sending a furious telegram on 8 April. 'I leave you with the indelible disgrace of abandoning the garrisons ... the climax of meanness.' This was leaked to the press, which was greatly excited by Gordon's plight. Gladstone turned down Gordon's request for Indian and British troop reinforcements. Later in April, the telegraph was cut, but Gordon could still get messages through by runner.

Gladstone was reluctant to act. He complained to the Queen that the Government had to take decisions at short notice on 'a peculiar, remote and more than half-barbarous region' with which it had 'but a very slight and indirect connection.' But in September 1884 Sir Garnet Wolseley, another China veteran, was put in command of a force to relieve Gordon.

Wolseley was in no great hurry. The Mahdi's forces had time to wait for the Nile flood to abate, before attacking Khartoum from the river. They broke in, slaughtering the garrison and killing Gordon on 26 January, 1885. Two days later Wolseley's advance guard reached the city. Gordon had been decapitated, and his head hung in a tree.

The news reached London on 5 February. The Queen vented her anger in a telegram to Gladstone: '... to think that all this might have been prevented ... by earlier action'. Gordon was seen as a martyr. But far from being a set-back to empire, his death became a spur. It was avenged in 1898, when Sir Horatio Kitchener crushed the Mahdi's successor at the battle of Omdurman. The young Winston Churchill saw action with the Lancers.

'Pax Britannica'

The decade saw new British protectorates created in North Bechuanaland, New Guinea, Matabeleland, Sarawak, Brunei and North Borneo. Upper Burma and Zululand were annexed. The Queen opened the Imperial and Colonial Exhibition in London in 1886, useful for the public to get a better idea of the exotic places now ruled in their name.

The Indian National Congress was founded the same year, an event of great future significance, but scarcely noticed at a time when J R Seeley's *The Expansion*

of England reflected the home nation's self-confidence. The 'great fact' of modern English history, Seeley said, was the spread of English-speaking people to all the corners of the globe. The empire, he said in a much-quoted phrase, had been acquired 'in a fit of absence of mind'. It was not Roman, not militaristic, but maritime and trading; the mother country was not authoritarian, but free. He saw Britain as a 'world-Venice, with the sea for streets'. The Queen found the book 'admirable … so statesmanlike, so farsighted, clear and fair'.

Why did the empire spread? The Earl of Derby gave the Queen several reasons why part of New Guinea should become a British protectorate. None was conclusive in itself: the Australians wanted it, Bismarck had ambitions for Germany in the Pacific, and it was the best way of protecting the natives from the 'lawless acts committed by adventurers of all countries'.

This last – the belief in empire as a civilising force for good – underpinned the expansive urge and gave it a moral gloss. It was a view held by Liberals as well as Conservatives and, far from being reactionary, was seen as progressive. Trade (if not in slaves or alcohol), the Christian religion and British administration were held to be universally good. Indeed, in some cases, the order and peacefulness that the British generally kept – when not employed in punitive expeditions, which the soldiers called 'butcher and bolt' missions – was preferred by many to the brutality and backwardness from which they had escaped.

GENERAL EXPERIENCE
'Everything's Sir Garnet', meaning 'all's well', was a phrase that lasted as long as the memory of General Garnet Wolseley lingered in the British mind. He is seen here aboard ship with his staff officers around him in 1885. In 50 years of soldiering, he campaigned across the world: few if any generals have fought in so many far-flung campaigns. He was wounded in Burma and the Crimea. He fought in India from 1857 to 1859, including at the siege of Lucknow. He commanded the British in the Anglo-French expedition to China in 1860. Posted to Canada he observed the American Civil War, and put down the Red River rebellion in 1870. He commanded the expedition to Ashanti, followed by stints in Cyprus and South East Africa. In 1882 he commanded at the battle of Tel el-Kebir in Egypt. But he arrived too late to save General Gordon at Khartoum in 1885. He was commander in chief of the army from 1890 to 1895, and mobilised forces for the Boer War in 1899.

A mural in the Foreign Office showed 'Britannica Pacificatrix' maintaining the peace for her subject peoples. It included a Biblical quotation: 'For thou shalt judge the folk righteously and govern the nations upon the earth.' A little later, Sylvia Leith-Ross, an Englishwoman, saw the result in the flesh. She was riding to join her husband in northern Nigeria when she came across a line of women, walking along the grassy track, lightly, securely, singing softly. The Englishman with her reined in his pony, and said simply: 'Pax Britannica'. For ever after, she said, though colonialism had come to be seen as exploitation by some, 'I would think of these women, who because of England could walk safely through the bush, singing'. The Queen shared this sense of protection. Fearing that Gladstone was ready to quit Sudan, she told him furiously that it would be a 'disgrace' if the Sudanese were 'left a prey to murder and rapine and utter confusion'.

No such fine instincts, of course, were held by the men trading Indian opium for Chinese gold and porcelain, or paying for West African palm oil with gin, or flocking to the Transvaal after gold was found there in 1886. For those whose health held out, and for those at home who supported them, there was money and glory to be carved out of empire.

The scramble for Africa

Lord Salisbury said that when he left the Foreign Office in 1880 no one had spared a thought for Africa. When he returned five years later, no one talked of anything else. There was no master plan. 'The conquests … are forced upon us,' the *Manchester Guardian* complained in 1884. There were many partial reasons for the rush – European powers were jealous of one another, unwilling to see a rival steal a lead; they wanted raw materials and new markets; quinine now checked malaria, making Africa less of a white man's grave – but perhaps the most important was that Africa was a vacuum, perceived as backward. It had no written languages, and not even the wheel. It seemed easy pickings.

The Portuguese, the original colonisers, had been followed by the British and French. When the Germans and Belgians joined in, *The Times* coined the phrase 'the scramble for Africa' in September 1884. An international conference opened in Berlin two months later to settle conflicting claims. British claims along the lower Niger, and German ones in Togoland and the Cameroons, were recognised. France was awarded Upper Niger and Gabon. King Leopold of the Belgians, who spoke of Africa as a 'magnificent cake', was the big winner. His private enterprise company was awarded a vast tract of the Congo, which it would cruelly exploit.

It was typical that Gladstone, an anti-imperialist, should unwittingly preside over a colossal expansion of empire. 'Terribly have I been puzzled and perplexed on finding a group of the soberest men among us to have concocted a scheme such as that touching the mountain country behind Zanzibar,' he said, referring to Mount Kilimanjaro. The habit of extending the empire to forestall others doing so gathered momentum. The public approved:

Wider still and wider, shall thy bounds be set!
God that made thee mighty – make thee mightier yet!

TEA AND SOAP
Trade always underpinned the Empire and Thomas Lipton was a classic example of how the empire could reward a hard-working entrepreneur. He began his working life as a nine-year-old errand boy in Glasgow, then went to America when he was 15, working on tobacco plantations and in a grocer's. He returned in 1870, aged 20, and opened his first grocer's shop in Glasgow. By 1880 he was a youthful millionaire, and was buying tea plantations in Ceylon. He grew his own tea, picked it, packed it, transported it and sold it in his own shops. The rather tongue-in-cheek advert for Pears soap below appeared in 1884 during the Sudan crisis. It illustrates the other side of the trading coin: selling British products around the empire.

AFRICAN PLAYER
H M Stanley, seen (left) with an ingeniously air-conditioned hat, was one of the great Victorian adventurer-journalists. He was born in Wales, but sailed off to New Orleans as a cabin boy. He fought in the American Civil War, and became a reporter for the *New York Herald*, where he was given the laconic assignment: 'Find Livingstone'. This he did, and today is chiefly remembered for the famous phrase, 'Dr Livingstone, I presume', with which he greeted the great explorer and missionary. But Stanley went on to play a bigger and darker role in Victorian Africa. As the European 'scramble' accelerated, he took a commission from King Leopold II of Belgium to help carve out a private empire that eventually became the Congo Free State. In 1887, when this picture was taken (right), Stanley (second from right) was in Zanzibar on his way to relieve Emin Pasha, a German doctor and explorer who had become a powerful figure east of Lake Victoria. Along the way, the expedition discovered Lake Edward and Mount Ruwenzori.

Gladstone might say that he welcomed a 'colonial' Germany as 'our ally and partner in the execution of the great purposes of Providence for the advantage of Mankind'. Others were not so sure that Bismarck had Providence in mind with regard to Germany's new possessions in Africa and the Pacific: they preferred Britain to get there first. The new lands were a hodgepodge of colonies, protectorates, territories and dependencies: Ascension Island in mid-Atlantic was treated as a naval vessel, with a Captain RN as governor. The imperial red on the map lapped into Somaliland, northern Borneo, eastern New Guinea, Nigeria and Bechuanaland. It coloured Pacific islands.

The expansion into Africa produced brave men and martyrs, men like James Hannington, who was appointed Anglican bishop of the newly created diocese of Eastern Equatorial Africa in 1884. Hannington was 37 when, in January 1885, he set off for his new diocese. A steamer dropped him off at Mombassa, and he began the trek to Uganda. By October he had reached Lake Victoria-Nyanza, where he was seized by the King of Ganda, Mwanga, who was alarmed to find a white man so far from the coast. Mwanga was influenced by powerful Muslim slave traders, who had no desire to see a Christian bishop and abolitionist succeed. 'Was held up by the 30th Psalm, which came with great power', he wrote on 29 October. 'A hyena howled near me last night, smelling a sick man. I hope it is not to have me yet.' It was his last day in captivity. He was killed, with his own gun, and all but four of the 50 men with him were speared to death.

After the Hannington murder, Uganda was in chaos as Protestant and French Catholic missionaries vied with one another and with Muslim slavers. Frederick Lugard was a soldier who had served in India. Both his parents were missionaries, and he resigned from the Indian Army after an unhappy love affair, then devoted himself to the missionary African Lakes Company. He ranged around the shores of Lake Nyasa, fighting the Arab and Swahili slavers who made regular forays into

DIAMOND WEALTH

A young boy named Erasmus Jacobs found a diamond near the banks of the Orange River in 1867. He was a Boer, an Afrikaans-speaking descendant of the first white settlers in the Cape. It was called the 'Eureka diamond', for it was the first indication that southern Africa was a storehouse of precious stones and metals. At first, the discovery was thought a fluke, but when the 83-carat 'Star of Africa' diamond was found nearby, a diamond rush began. It centred on the Kimberley mine, where these men (right) are sorting diamonds in 1885. Many of the newcomers were English-speakers. They included Cecil Rhodes, an 18-year-old lad from Bishop's Stortford in Hertfordshire, an imperialist and mining entrepreneur of genius. The British promptly annexed Griqualand West, the area that included the diamond fields. Tensions eventually erupted in the First Boer War in 1880-1, which led to the Boer republics of the Transvaal and Orange Free State gaining near-independence from the British Empire.

GOLD MINES

The discovery in 1884 of a vast goldfield on the Witwatersrand in the Transvaal soon sucked in thousands of British miners and prospectors. The city of Johannesburg was created virtually overnight. These white and African miners were photographed panning for gold on the surface in 1888. Soon, mines were being sunk thousands of feet into the ground. The temperature rises only 9°C for each 1,000m of depth on the Rand, where in most mines it rises by 25°C. The political temperature, alas, was meteoric. The British had tolerated the Boer republics while they were poor and agricultural. But the Rand was now one of the world's most fabulous money-making machines, and the British feared for their supremacy in the rest of south Africa. These tensions helped to stoke the Second Boer War.

Nyasaland. Badly wounded in 1888, he was then commissioned by the Imperial British East Africa Company to consolidate its interests in Uganda. This he did, journeying far up-country through the Ruwenzori Mountains, recruiting 600 Sudanese soldiers, then marching back south to force King Mwanga and his followers to flee to an island in the lake, and massacring them. 'The curse of Africa and of Uganda in especial is guns,' Lugard wrote.

Cecil Rhodes, son of a Hertfordshire parson, was a 17 year old when he arrived on the east coast of Africa in 1870. Within three years, he was a major entrepreneur in the fabulous diamond mine at Kimberley: he owned the ice-making plant, imported mining and construction equipment, bringing heavy pumps and engines 600 miles from Cape Town by ox wagon, and had the water-pumping contract for the whole mine. In 1886, gold was discovered at Witwatersrand near Pretoria. By 1887, he controlled De Beers Mining and the Kimberley mines, and would soon form Consolidated Goldfields.

As tin and lead mining slumped at home, thousands of miners from Cornwall and elsewhere emigrated to the goldfields of South Africa and Australia. Dispossessed Highlanders and Irishmen, and farm labourers caught up by the collapse in cereal prices, joined the scores of thousands who each year made the empire their new home. Just getting there needed a strong constitution. A Scot emigrating to Canada described going below as his ship left Greenock. 'Some were groaning in their berths, others lying on the floor, others retching incessantly,' he recalled. 'I could not sleep, for as the gale increased, so did the noises within and without. I could hear the heavy wind whistling mournfully through the damp, tight-drawn cordage, and the waves breaking in successive showers on the deck overhead … As the storm gained upon us, the ship laboured more and heavily, until everything movable in steerage rolled about the floor from side to side.' But the age had character in plenty. There were many takers.

WHAT OF THOSE WHO REMAINED?

Compared to the Scots and Irish, who packed the emigrant boats, the Welsh were not great emigrants. This was in part, perhaps, because they had more sense of their own identity, particularly as expressed through their language. At the time of the 1891 census more than half of the Welsh could speak Welsh, with 30 per cent speaking nothing else. (Only 1.2 per cent of the Irish spoke just Irish, with 17 per cent bilingual, and a bare 6 per cent of Scots spoke Gaelic.) A society to increase the use of Welsh in schools was founded in 1885, and bans on using Welsh in the classroom were lifted in 1888.

Gladstone was little concerned with the principality politically, but he lived in Wales – at Hawarden in Flintshire – and pronounced it a nation during a speech at Swansea in 1887. He also supported the Welsh Sunday Closing Bill, to the annoyance of the brewers. The Welsh did a great deal for Gladstone. His strain of Liberalism – favourable to dissent and the rights of small nationalities – was reflective of the ideals of chapel-goers and suited them admirably. Most of them voted for him: the Liberals took all but four of the 43 Welsh seats in the 1885 election. They remained loyal to him on Home Rule, too, unlike the Scots, who made plain their dislike of Irish immigrants and Catholicism. Even a young firebrand like David Lloyd George, first returned as a Liberal MP in 1886, made no play with independence. The Queen visited the principality in 1889, sympathising with 'this naturally sensitive and warm-hearted people' that the Prince of Wales could not be prised away from London to come himself.

Church and chapel-goers

The Welsh were the greatest church-goers in Britain. The best equipped, too: their churches and chapels could seat more than three quarters of the Welsh population, against just half in England. Indeed, little Aberdaron in Caernarfon could seat all of its 1,239 people and still find room for 300 visitors. The principality was peppered

WELSH TRADITION
A Welsh family demonstrating traditional crafts of spinning and knitting at Betws-y-Coed. Although the picture is clearly posed, as part of a series on local costumes, the Welsh did retain a strong sense of their national identity. Love for the Welsh language was seen in the chapels and at Eisteddfods celebrating Welsh music and poetry. Wales was the Land of Song, made so not by cliché but by the male voice choirs of the pit villages and ironworks. Their great anthem was 'Hen Wlad Fy Nhadau' ('Land of my Fathers'). 'It is wonderful how well these choirs sing,' Queen Victoria said as she listened to them on her visit in 1889.

COTTAGE INDUSTRY

An Irishman weaves a length of tweed on a hand loom in Donegal in 1880. The home weaving industry was the mainstay of the eonomy in many remote communities, the most famous product being Harris tweed from the islands of the Outer Hebrides. In general the Irish were less conscious of their Celtic language and culture than the Welsh. One reason for this was the suppression of the Irish language in the school system, but a greater cause was the long history of emigration. The Irish had been leaving in huge numbers for much of the century. By the 1880s an attempt to bolster Irish ethnicity was underway, with the growth of Gaelic games. The Gaelic Athletic Association was founded in 1884.

with chapels with fine Biblical names: Hebron, Zion, Ebenezer, Calfaria or Calvary. These, with Sabbatarianism, temperance and regard for education and the Welsh language were 'pillars of godly righteousness'. Yet, oddly, registry office weddings were more common than anywhere in England.

'In dealing with Wales,' the MP for Denbighshire, Osborne Morgan, told the Commons, 'you are really dealing with an entirely distinct nationality.' And so it was, but there were few stirrings for independence. The nationalism of Cymru Fydd, founded in 1886, was cultural more than political. One reason for this, and for the survival of Welsh as a language, was because times were never so bad as to force large-scale emigration, as it had for the Gaelic-speaking Highlanders and down-trodden, impoverished Irish.

The state of Scotland

Glasgow had been hit by a severe financial crisis in 1878. Its magnificent City Chambers, which the Queen inaugurated in 1888, were conceived to restore Glasgow's civic and commercial morale and to underpin its claim to be the 'Second City of Empire'. William Young designed a great Italianate tower to dominate the exterior in a whirl of Flemish, French and Venetian motifs. The grand staircase and reception rooms glowed with marble, mahogany and ceramic tiles, with rich stained glass, murals and alabaster friezes.

The city still exuded the self-confidence of Scottish insurance, banking, shipping, mines, engineering and shipbuilding works. The apex of this was Templeton's Carpet Factory in Glasgow, designed in 1889 by William Leiper to show that an industrial building could delight the eye. The owners declared their intent 'as patrons of the arts, resolved not alone in the interests of the workers, but also of the citizens, to erect instead of the ordinary and common factory something of permanent architectural interest and beauty'. It had soaring towers, battlements, loggias and balustrades, in Venetian Gothic and Romanesque, with mosaics and multi-coloured brickwork.

Scotland's cities might display civic pride, but the story in the Highlands was very different. The crofters suffered high rents, insecure tenure and eviction at landlords' hands, treatment as harsh as anything in Ireland, and they began to respond in the same way, forming a Highland Land League which returned four Crofter candidates in the 1885 elections. The next year, the passing of the Crofters' Act meant they need no longer fear eviction, at least in the seven 'crofting counties' of Shetland, Ross and Cromarty, Orkney, Caithness, Sutherland, Inverness and Argyll. In 1892 the Crofters merged with the Liberals. The movement was over, without having become nationalist.

The industrial south of Scotland was sharply distinct from the Highlands, and closer to England in conditions. Just 6 per cent of Scots spoke Gaelic – for centuries, the great majority had spoken Scots, the dialect of English found in the poems of Robert Burns. Scotland was overwhelmingly Liberal, with only anti-Catholicism to give the Tories a wisp of support. A few concessions were made. A memorial was raised in 1881 at Culloden, where the Duke of Cumberland had destroyed the Jacobites, to the memory of the 'brave Clans who fought for SCOTLAND and PRINCE CHARLIE' [original capitals]. The Scottish Office was set up by the government in 1885. But there was no pressure for Home Rule.

Hardship in rural England

In England, the decade brought particular hardships to country people. Wheat and wool had been the foundations of their prosperity since the Middle Ages. Both were buffeted by cheap imports. Almost the whole of Europe protected local farmers from cheap corn imports with tariff barriers. Britain and Belgium were the only exceptions. As the price of shipping grain from Chicago to Liverpool plummeted – down 300 per cent over the late 1870s and early 1880 – and the bread on city tables was milled from the abundance of the prairies, so the prices paid to English wheat farmers collapsed. By 1885, a million acres of farmland had come out of wheat production. Britain was importing 65 per cent of its wheat.

Competition was looming for livestock, too. The SS *Strathleven* arrived in Britain in February 1880 with the first cargo of frozen Australian meat. Two years later, frozen New Zealand lamb was carried aboard the *Dunedin*. It was good news for consumers in the towns, of course. The cost of the average family's weekly food basket fell by almost a third between 1877 and 1889, helped further by the development of cheap margarine and better food retailing.

A HARD LIFE

In a prize-winning photograph taken in early spring 1887, a farm worker takes a breather, leaning on his plough, while his team of horses stand patiently by. The 1880s were not a happy decade for British farming. With no protection from cheap imports and shipping costs falling dramatically, wheat and wool, the traditional staples of the rural economy, were ravaged. Australia and New Zealand had splendid sheep country in such plenty that they undercut local wool despite having to haul their produce half way round the world.

As for livestock, the arrival of the first consignment of frozen Australian meat was a harbinger of what was to come. A Queenslander, Thomas McIlwraith, chartered the steamer *Strathleven* and had it fitted out with Glasgow-made air compression/expansion refrigeration equipment. The ship was loaded in Melbourne with a trial shipment of frozen carcases and kegs of butter. It arrived in London on 2 February, 1880. The meat was in excellent condition and sold well.

'We labourers had no lack of lords and masters. There were the parson and his wife at the rectory. There was the squire … [who] lorded it right feudally over his tenants, the farmers. The farmers in their turn tyrannised over the labourers.'

Joseph Arch MP, former agricultural labourer

THE QUEEN'S NAMESAKE

Named to commemorate the Queen's Jubilee, the handsome but ill-fated HMS *Victoria* steams proudly down the River Tyne shortly after being launched in 1887. She was the first battleship to have triple expansion steam engines. She was built by Armstrong Whitworth, major shipbuilders on Tyneside, and could make just under 17 knots. She was armed with two 16.25 inch guns, as well as 6-inch and 10-inch guns. Only two of these Victoria or Sans Pareil class battleships were ever built. HMS *Victoria* herself was sunk in a collision with HMS *Camperdown* during manoeuvres in the Mediterranean in 1893, and 358 of her 630-man crew were lost.

Proving that it never rains but it pours, farmers were also hit by the weather. The four years to 1882 were exceptionally wet, creating perfect conditions for outbreaks of liver-rot among sheep in the West Country and Lincolnshire marshes. Foot-and-mouth and rinderpest ravaged the cattle. Impoverished country folk left for the towns and colonies. Life was tough for those who stayed, as the MP Joseph Arch, a former agricultural worker, recalled. 'At the sight of the squire people trembled … labourers were no better than toads under a harrow.'

The county set and landed estates

Ironically, this was a golden period for the county and country house set. 'The county' was the rural hierarchy. The lord lieutenant was at its head, and beneath him came the MFHs – Masters of Foxhounds – the landed gentry, the bishop chairman of the quarter sessions, the colonel of the county yeomanry, the MPs, the dean, the Justices of the Peace, and the lesser clergy and bigger farmers.

Taxation had not yet broken up the great estates. Death duties provided a little over 8 per cent of public revenue, itself so slim as to be all but unrecognisable in today's terms. Land, property and income taxes accounted for a further 17 per cent. After holdings of less than an acre are excluded, just 1,200 people owned a quarter of the land. These were the truly rich, with an average of 16,200 acres. A further quarter was in the hands of 6,200 landowners, each with some 3,000 acres. The largest estates were in the North and West. High land prices near the cities had tempted people to sell land for urban development over the years.

It was prodigiously expensive to run a great country house and even some of the grandest families were feeling the pinch. The Duke of Marlborough had to sell off the Blenheim enamels for £73,000 in 1882. Standards had to be maintained, and, at least in terms of staff, they were higher than ever. Some servants were employed simply to serve other servants. T F Buxton, the owner of Easneyer near Ware in Hertfordshire, had 23 servants and reckoned that 15 waited on the family, and eight on the 15. Servants were kept out of sight as much as possible. The servants' quarters at Mentmore Towers, the Rothschilds' colossal new house in Buckinghamshire, were almost as large as the mansion itself, but the building was blank stone on the exterior. The only windows looked onto an inner courtyard, so that the servants could not glimpse their employers, nor vice versa.

At Stoke Rochford Hall, Lincolnshire, newly built for landowner Christopher Turnor, the architect William Burn gave each household department its own set of rooms. The butler, with five menservants under him, was in the basement under the main house. This gave the footmen easy access to the hall and front door. The housekeeper had four housemaids, two still-room maids for the pantry and three laundry maids, and they lodged beneath the family part of the house. The kitchen department, in the kitchen court, was staffed by a cook, two kitchen maids, a scullery maid and a dairy maid. It was almost 50 yards from the kitchen to the dining room. Better that a footman have a long walk than the dining room be tainted by kitchen smells, above all cabbage water, which the gentility abhorred.

Eaton Hall, the Duke of Westminster's home, had 50 indoor servants. The agent was the main figure of the household, responsible for repairs and maintenance, collecting rents and generally running the estate, a task that might involve mining rights, transport and housing developments. The Duke of Bedford paid his agent £1,800 a year, as much as a senior railway manager. Beneath him, the Steward was responsible for male staff – the butler, footmen, grooms, coachmen, gamekeepers, gardeners, valets and pages. The housekeeper did the same for the women staff – the cooks, housemaids, scullery maids, chambermaids and ladies' maids, the latter ideally Frenchwomen.

As the farming slump bit, the nouveaux riches outbuilt the hereditary landowners by two to one in country houses. The money came from biscuits, with G W Palmer's Marlstone House in Berkshire, from soap, in Robert Hudson's Danesfield in Buckinghamshire, or beer, like James Watney's Haling Park in Surrey.

Modesty and sexual reality

For all the extravagance of the Victorian grandee, Queen Victoria brought to court, and to the nation, a prim and middle-class morality far from such aristocratic excess. Marriage was sacrosanct: until 1887, even the innocent parties in divorce were barred from the royal court. Divorce was an extreme rarity. Only four marriages in 10,000 ended in it, the lowest rate of any Western country in which statistics were kept. Many resorted to mistresses, lovers and prostitutes. A duchess, the Fabian Beatrice Webb remarked, could exchange 'her insignificant duke for a powerful marquis as a habitual companion without causing the slightest dent in her social acceptability'. It was not so easy further down the social scale, but as long as word did not blatantly get out no disgrace ensued.

It was the same with homosexuality. Sodomy and 'unnatural misdemeanours' were criminal offences – the law was tightened in 1885 to make sodomy a felony punishable by up to 10 years penal servitude – but there were only some 100 committals a year in England and Wales. In practice, homosexuality was on an altogether greater scale than these figures suggest: London, in particular, had many male prostitutes and homosexual brothels. Little action was taken, though.

The illegitimacy rate was about 4.8 per cent, where it remained until the 1960s and the advent of the Pill and legalised abortion. The birth rate began to slow in the 1880s: couples who married in the 1860s averaged over six children, and this fell to a little over four. It cannot be told how much this was due to abortion. Prosecutions for attempting to procure a miscarriage were rarer still than those for homosexuality: just 15 committals in all England and Wales in 1883.

Family allowances and child benefit did not exist, and children were a responsibility rarely taken on before husband and wives were in their twenties. Miners, male factory workers and textile hands were typically 24 when they married, their wives one or two years younger. Artisans and labourers were a year older, clerks and shopkeepers 26. There was then a jump, to farmers and farmers' sons, who typically married at 29 to women a year younger than themselves. The professional and independent classes averaged 31 when they married, though their wives were a good five years younger.

Religion – a social force

Religion was part of the social fabric. Both the Prime Ministers of the decade were religious men. Gladstone felt on his election in 1880 that 'the Almighty has employed me for His purposes in a manner larger or more special than before'. Salisbury was a great reader of theology. Church patronage was still one of the Prime Minister's gifts. 'A vacant see is a great excitement to Mr G', his private secretary noted in 1884. 'I believe it excites him far more than a political crisis.'

Ideas were moulded by the lecture, periodical, book and pulpit. Religion was a great educator for those who had left school at 13 or earlier. 'Chapel meant

IN SUNDAY BEST
A church outing to Burnham Beeches in around 1887. For ordinary folk, the churches were the main source of entertainment. In addition to the usual services they organised Bands of Hope, Boys' Brigades, Girls' Friendly Brigades, festivals and outings for their congregations. Two thirds of the Church halls that still stand around the country were built in a great burst in the 1880s. They hosted concerts, lectures, nativity plays, competitions and good cheer to villages and towns. They were a natural site for meetings of the fledgling Mothers' Union, brainchild of Mary Sumner following the birth of her granddaughter in 1876. By the end of the century this organisation to support young mothers of all social classes had 150,000 members.

everything', a woman said of her father. 'There he was taught to read, was lent books. It was his only contact with education, its pulpit his only means of self-expression.' At least a quarter of the magazines published had a religious theme and 15 per cent of books were categorised as 'theology, sermons, Biblical'.

Britain had more clergymen per head of population than 'priest-ridden' Ireland, more than any European country but Spain and Italy. This was partly because there were so many denominations: Primitive Methodists, Presbyterians, Bible Christians, Plymouth Brethren, Quakers, Mormons and Seventh Day Adventists, Baptists, Anglicans, Catholics and more. These in turn supported Church-based thrift and temperance societies, debating clubs, sports teams, penny banks, literary and debating clubs, youth groups, Sunday schools, excursions, fetes and festivals, including Harvest Festivals, a popular 19th-century invention.

This was a revivalist age, a time of Salvation Army marches, great Wesleyan rallies, Catholic missions and fire-and-brimstone sermons. The sermon was live

'Chapel meant everything', a woman said of her father. 'It was his only contact with education'

entertainment, and evangelical preachers did not skimp, some considering 90 minutes to be an ideal length. John James, of Carr Lane Independent Chapel in Birmingham, could keep going for hours on end, topping up his energy by sucking oranges tossed up to him by friends below the pulpit. The Salvation Army grew at staggering pace, from 50 corps and 88 officers in 1878, to 1,006 corps and 2,260 officers in 1886. It put across its temperance message with enough effect to rattle the brewers and publicans, who hired gangs of louts, the Skeleton Army, to attack Salvation Army parades. The American revivalists Dwight Moody and Ira Sankey, firm favourites following a tour of Britain in the mid-1870s, returned in 1888. Moody preached and Sankey sang well-crafted songs that comforted those who had lost dear ones with the certain promise of families reunited in heaven.

There was plenty of Anglican church-building and restoration in the 1880s – as well as the creation of new dioceses in Newcastle, Wakefield, Liverpool, Southwell – but the chapel-builders were the most active. Baptists, Methodists and Congregationalists were flourishing in commerce and manufacturing. Colman's

LANDMARK SPIRES
Only the castle competed with the church spires in the skyline of Inverness in 1880 (below). Oxford was famous as the home of 'dreaming spires', but church towers and spires were the most prominent landmarks the length and breadth of the nation in these pre-high rise days. Travellers could navigate by them, and foxhunters went 'steeplechasing' across the country, thus creating 'point to point' racing. Many new churches and spires were added to the British landscape in Victorian times, and many existing ones were restored.

mustard, Crossley's soups, Leverhulme soaps, Salt's cloths were all businesses founded by Nonconformists. Quakers had wealthy industrialists, too: the Bryants of Bryant & May matches, the Palmers of Huntley & Palmer biscuits, the cocoa and chocolate-making Cadburys, Rowntrees and Frys, the shoemaking Clarkes. There were the Unitarians and Old Dissenters, and the newfangled Mormons.

Missionaries, immigrants and refugees

Brigham Young, who created Salt Lake City, and partly populated it with children by his many wives, was the first Mormon missionary to Britain in 1840. He baptized 8,000 people, claiming: 'We gather those who are poor, who wish to be redeemed, who feel the oppression the high and the proud have made them endure.' The brave and desperate poor responded to the extraordinary polygamous message of the Mormons and the call of the American frontier. Some Mormons stayed in Britain, but most emigrated. Since the first group sailed from Liverpool in 1840 thousands of British Mormons had joined the migrations to 'the Land of Zion'. Other American sects followed. The first overseas mission of the Adventists arrived in Southampton in 1878 and was modestly successful. On Pitcairn Island, remotest outpost of the Empire in the Pacific, Adventists won over all the inhabitants, descendants of Christian Fletcher and the mutineers from the *Bounty*.

The Irish boosted the numbers of Catholics in Britain, particularly in Scotland, where the 1881 census showed 218,000 people, 6 per cent of the population, were Irish born. In England and Wales they made up a little over 2 per cent, though this was 562,000 people. A considerable church-building programme was needed to cope. By 1890, the number of Catholic churches had reached 1,335, up from 586 in 1850. The number of priests had tripled to 2,478. They were known for their work among the poor. This, too, was largely because of the Irish, for whom the priests were a welcome and stabilising reminder of home. Memories were fading of the 1850 anti-Catholic riots in Liverpool, Birkenhead and elsewhere, but Fenian bombs and murders reignited feelings against the Irish and their religion, which the Conservatives were adept at tapping into and turning against Home Rule.

Substantial numbers of Jews arrived after each new anti-Jewish pogrom broke out in Poland, the Ukraine and other parts of the Russian empire. By 1881, they numbered about 60,000. Jewish emancipation in Britain had followed that of Catholics but almost 30 years later, in 1858.

Religious differences

Beliefs were often fervently held, and little love was lost between sects. Protestants feared Catholic growth, the revival of Jesuits and the influx of the Irish. Catholics were split between the Ultramontanes, like Henry Manning, archbishop of Westminster and Anglican convert, who supported the dogma of papal infallibility, and those less deferential to the pope, like Cardinal Newman. Old practices – such as advowson, the buying and selling of the right to present an Anglican benefice – died hard. Pews were still rented and reflected a worshipper's social standing. The Wesleyan Park Chapel in Sheffield charged 9 shillings and sixpence for the front row, 8 shillings for the second, 6 shillings and sixpence for the third and so on back to 3 shillings for corner seats.

Wealth and status were reflected, too, in clergy income. Anglicans were by far the best-heeled. Best educated, too, even if Oxford and Cambridge were no longer quite the Anglican assembly lines they once were. Their vicarages and rectories were among the most beautiful and comfortable homes in the country. The average annual stipend had reached £275 in 1840. It had fallen slightly since then, at least for the country clergy, whose income from tithes had begun falling with the agricultural depression in the mid-1870s. In contrast a Nonconformist minister might be little better off than a labourer, with £36 a year. Catholic priests, without wives and children to support, might have as little as £25 and board and housing.

THE SLOW BIRTH OF SOCIALISM

Marxism had famously scorned religion as the 'opium of the people'. Karl Marx himself died in 1883 and was buried in Highgate Cemetery in London, but his Socialist ideas now began to reach influential people in Britain. George Bernard Shaw, a young Irish dramatist, essayist and vegetarian, read Marx and developed what he called his 'kindly dislike' of capitalist society. Shaw was one of the first members of the Fabian Society, founded in 1884. So was the remarkable Annie Besant.

The Fabians' aim was to promote socialism, not through revolution, but by encouraging its growth from existing British society. It was a slow process. The members of all socialist groups had barely reached 3,000 in the mid-1880s, when the Tories' newly-minted Primrose League had reached 250,000 and was climbing fast. The Russian anarchist Prince Pyotr Kropotkin, who settled in Britain in 1886, found himself lecturing to 'ridiculously small audiences … For me, who held advanced socialist opinions, there was no atmosphere to breath in.'

Nonetheless, Henry Hyndman had founded the Democratic Federation in 1881 after reading Marx. Hyndman was an Old Etonian. He wore a silk hat and frock coat, and carried a silver-topped cane, but he called his Federation colleagues and working class people 'Comrades'. An early recruit was William Morris, painter, designer, poet, novelist, publisher, tapestry weaver, architect and businessman, another all-rounder alive with the energy of the day.

Morris, like Hyndman, was a public school and Oxbridge socialist, whose beliefs were based on an emotional rejection of industry and mass production. A deep admiration for medieval craftsmanship suffused his work. His woodblock printed textiles and wallpapers are popular designs still produced and sold today. 'One must

CLEANING UP
A soap warehouse in Lambeth in London. Small-scale manufacture of staples like soap was already under threat from mass production. William Lever, the son of a Bolton grocer, began making soap from vegetable oils instead of tallow in 1886. When he relocated his factory to Merseyside, he founded a model town in 1888 to give his workforce an ideal community. Port Sunlight, as Lever's new town was called, was utterly removed from the Lambeth slums. It was a bright and airy place, full of green spaces, and neat houses with vernacular details, such as cross-bands of brick and gabled windows.

BIG GUNS
The breech block of a heavy gun being gauged and fitted at the Royal Arsenal in Woolwich in 1885. The huge site in southeast London, on the south bank of the Thames, had been used as an ordnance storage depot since the 17th century, and a gun foundry was set up in 1717. Much of the military sinew of the Empire was manufactured or developed here at Woolwich. It had important laboratories as well as ordnance factories and gun foundries. A year after this picture was taken, the Woolwich workers started their own football club, which flourishes today north of the river as Arsenal.

turn to hope', Morris said of socialism. It offered a 'definite conception of a new order'. He joined the Federation because 'it is the only active socialist organisation in England'. It soon splintered. Morris and others left to form the Socialist League at the end of 1884, only to move on again three years later when it fell into the hands of anarchists.

Anarchists and rioters gave early socialism a poor image. Morris himself was caught up in brawling in February 1886 when Socialist League orators stirred up a crowd of 10,000 marching from Trafalgar Square to Hyde Park protesting about unemployment. As they passed the gentlemen's clubs of Pall Mall and St James's, they hurled paving stones and metal railings as club servants pelted them with rubbish and dustbin lids. Another ill-tempered meeting in Hyde Park held a year later saw the crowd spill across Park Lane and move on to smash windows in Oxford Street. The window displays of carpets, wallpapers and fabrics at No 449 escaped – they were the showrooms of Morris & Co.

Spencer's attack

Socialism was still on the fringes, with little mass appeal, and aroused little interest. Herbert Spencer, though, Darwin's old champion, was alarmed by the drift to collectivism. Anticipating the welfare state, he wrote a far-sighted attack on the increase in state meddling and regulation in *Man versus the State* in 1884.

Liberalism, he said, 'habitually stood for individual freedom against State coercion'. It had fought the notion of a monarch's unlimited authority. It should now dispute unlimited parliamentary authority. But it did not. Once, a man could spend his earnings as he pleased. Now, the government said, 'we will spend it for

MODERN INDUSTRY
Women at work in Birdsall's bookbinding business in Northampton in 1888. The company dated back to 1792 but came into its own under the management of the founder's great-great-nephew, Richard Birdsall, who enlarged and modernised the works in 1882 and again in 1888. Birdsall's beautifully bound editions of Dickens's complete works are still much sought after. Family firms like this, and their skilled women workers, were backbones of industry, but not all were fortunate enough to work for such enlightened employers.

the general benefit'. The 'welfare of the people' had become the supreme law, used to justify interference in every area of life: enforced vaccinations, load-lines on ships, bans on paying wages in pubs, compulsory education, the regulation of lodging houses, public baths, public transport … 'ever-multiplying coercive measures, each of which requires an additional staff of officers'.

A man who joined a Trade Union sacrificed his liberty to the collective. 'He is compelled to strike if a majority so decide', Spencer wrote, 'he is forbidden to accept work save under the conditions they dictate … He cannot disobey without bringing on himself the persecution and perhaps violence of his fellows.'

A new and vociferous notion held that 'all social suffering is removable, and that it is the duty of somebody or other to remove it'. Both these beliefs, he said, were false. London was full of 'good-for-nothings who in one way or another live on the good-for-somethings – vagrants and sots, criminals and those on the way to crime, youths who are burdens on hard-worked parents …' Why should they be helped? Was it not 'natural that they should bring unhappiness on themselves and those connected with them?'

Political effects of unemployment

But many had been forced to do nothing, when they would much rather do something. The depression had led to a huge rise in 'unemployment' – a freshly minted word – which helped the socialists to expand their support. A major demonstration against unemployment was held in November 1886. William Morris and Annie Besant led a march from Clerkenwell Green to Trafalgar Square. They linked up at Charing Cross station with the radical MP and writer R Cunninghame Graham and John Burns, a rough, tough South London trade unionist and brilliant orator.

Others were marching from Bermondsey. They were met on Westminster Bridge by massed police, backed by 400 Life Guards. The police, mounted and on foot, *The Times* correspondent reported, 'charged in among the people, striking indiscriminately in all directions … I witnessed several cases of injury to men who had been struck on the head or face by the police. The blood, in most instances, was flowing freely from the wounds and the spectacle was indeed a sickening one.'

A young protester, Alfred Linnell, died after a clash with police in another demonstration the following Sunday. Annie Besant stage-managed his funeral on 18 December. The cortege set off from Soho to the 'Dead March from Saul', with an open hearse and four horses. The coffin was emblazoned 'Killed in Trafalgar Square'. The pall bearers included Besant, William Morris, Cunninghame Graham and the crusading journalist W T Stead. The burial service was conducted by the Rev Stewart Headlam, a Christian Socialist. 'Their brother lay there', Morris wrote, 'let them remember for all time this man as their brother and their friend.' His hymn, 'A Death Song', was set to music by Malcolm Lawson and sung: 'Not me, nor thousands must they slay / But one and all if they would dusk the day …

Reformers from the Establishment

For all the patronising and posturing – the exquisite, refined, Marlborough-and-Oxford educated Morris standing beside the coffin of an obscure legal clerk and threatening apocalypse – it was significant that leading British reformers were so often born into the Establishment. Gladstone and Hyndman were Etonians. Two of the most effective reformers were Harrovians – Cardinal Manning, now busy with royal commissions on education and housing for the poor, and the incomparable Lord Shaftesbury. It was as a schoolboy at Harrow back in 1815 that Shaftesbury had seen a pauper's funeral, the body drunkenly exposed by the cackling vagrants carrying it, and decided there and then to devote himself 'to the cause of the weak, the helpless, both man and beast'.

Shaftesbury was still in harness, campaigning for child acrobats, when he died 70 years later. At his funeral in October 1885, thousands stood hatless, baring their heads in pouring rain to show their love and respect for him. The signs that some held – 'I was in prison and ye visited me', 'I was hungered and ye gave me meat' – were the literal truth, for he had sought out prisoners and the hungry. The famous statue at Piccadilly Circus is not Eros, as commonly believed. It is of his twin brother, Anteros, the God of Selfless Love, and it was placed there as a memorial to the great Victorian social reformer.

It meant much to the stability of the nation that a seventh earl should show such compassion. However watertight it seemed, the class system was permeable: it could be penetrated by conscience and ideals, without the need for violence and revolution. Marxism did not grip the imagination. Though John Burns was arrested and briefly imprisoned for incitement during the demonstrations, he and others like him sought to better the lot of the working man through Parliament.

Special forces

People were made nervous by the demonstrations in London and by Fenian bombings, as well as the presence of professional revolutionaries like Kropotkin. The first moves to set up a police department to monitor domestic and foreign trouble-makers were taken in 1881. It became known as the Special Branch in 1887, and drew on the experience of intelligence-gathering on the Fenians.

The novelist Henry James, an American resident in England, feared that the poor would rise from the black depths of their misery as 'Huns and vandals' to avenge themselves on the rich. Much of England, drawing its wealth and privilege from the 'sooty and besmirched landscape', he thought, 'is grossly materialistic and wants blood-letting'.

But the unions, with well-led strikes, proved capable of venting anger before it exploded. Skilled craftsmen had organised themselves since the medieval guilds, with apprenticeships and other regulations ensuring they remained masters of their trades. In the late 1880s, unskilled and casual workers began to get their own representatives for the first time. Unions were set up for dockers, matchmakers, gasworkers, railwaymen, seamen, miners and mill workers. Some went on strike, with enough effect to alarm employers, who themselves organised the better to resist them. Within a few years this would lead to the formation of the National Free Labour Association, which registered non-union workers and provided them to managements as strike-breakers.

Groundbreaking strikes

The Bryant & May match factory in London's East End was notorious for poisoning the women who worked there, for pay of just 5 shillings a week. 'Lucifer' matches filled the place with the dangerous fumes of yellow phosphorus, already banned in Sweden and America. The women ate in the factory, and so ingested the chemical as well as breathing the fumes. Annie Besant uncovered the horrors of working in the match factory with the help of three informants, who

GIRL POWER
Match girls from Bryant & May on strike in 1888. Bryant & May's factory in the East End of London may have been owned by Quakers, but it still had a grim reputation. The chemicals used, in particular yellow phosphorus, produced virulent skin and bone cancers. The faces of some of these girls already show the tell-tale swelling and deformation of 'phossy jaw'. As the women's teeth rotted they were pulled out by the factory foremen, one of them, Freddie Demuth, an illegitimate son of Karl Marx. In July 1888 Annie Besant, the radical feminist, announced that a Matchmakers' Union had been founded. She brought 1,400 women out on strike. Within three weeks, the management had conceded most of their demands for shorter hours, better pay and improved conditions. The Salvation Army opened its own match factory, using safer red phosphorus.

STRIKING FOR A LIVING WAGE
Onlookers watch from pavements and windows as a parade of London dockers progresses along the Strand during the Great Dock Strike of 1889. Union banners proclaim their struggle and 'No Surrender'. This was one of the first mass strikes in Britain, involving 30,000 men demanding a basic wage of sixpence an hour and a minimum of four hours work at a time. With no strike pay to fall back on, their families were saved from destitution by Salvation Army soup kitchens and donations from sympathisers as far away as Australia. It was a titanic test of wills between the dock owners and the workers, but after five long hard weeks, the strikers won. Ben Tillett (above left) led the strike, with help from John Burns (above right), a socialist who was later elected MP for Battersea.

were immediately sacked. In July 1888, Besant brought the women out on strike. Within three weeks the management conceded most of the demands.

Another new union, of Gasworkers and General Labourers, was formed in March 1889. It called a strike over conditions at Beckton Gas Works, with historic results. The workers won an eight-hour day. Only one in 20 workers was a member of a union, but the movement was growing.

The Great Dock Strike followed in August 1889. Dockers were paid piece rates and their income was precarious: when trade was slack, they earned nothing. Ben Tillett – a Bristol-born former circus acrobat and sailor, who became leader of the Docker's Union in London – wrote of the way dockers were hired each day, 'driven into a shed, iron-barred from end to end, outside of which a foreman or contractor walks up and down with the air of a dealer in a cattlemarket, picking and choosing from a crowd of men, who, in their eagerness to obtain employment, trample each other under foot, and … fight for the chances of a day's work.'

Tillett had to induce the solidarity and discipline for the men to stay out, with no money, for as long as it took. After four weeks, the strains were abundant, the men's families near destitute. Tillett was helped by Will Thorne, the gasworkers' leader, and by John Burns, instantly identifiable in a white straw hat and with a black beard. Burns was a master of morale-boosting demonstrations, with floats and carts and streaming Union banners. The men held firm. After five weeks, and with the help of Cardinal Manning acting as a skilful and powerful intermediary, the strikers won. The employment landscape of Britain had changed forever.

INDEX

Page numbers in *italic* refer to the captions.

PICTURE ACKNOWLEDGEMENTS

Abbreviations: t = top; m = middle; b = bottom; r = right; c = centre; l = left

All images in this book are courtesy of Getty Images, including the following which have additional attributions:
4, 30, 34r, 36-37, 43, 47, 70t, 107, 113, 115b, 116: Sean Sexton
17tl, 55tl, 92, 99, 106, 121l, 135b: Time & Life Pictures
19, 86l, 86m, 89t, 89bl: Bridgeman Art Library
28, 41: Robert Welch/Sean Sexton
39: Robert Banks/Sean Sexton
58-59, 61, 63mr, 64m, 64r, 65t, 66-67, 75b, 86r, 120, 131, 152, 156, 157r: Popperfoto
78r, 81b: Roger Viollet
130: Stock Montage

LOOKING BACK AT BRITAIN
EXPANSION OF EMPIRE – 1880s
is published by The Reader's Digest Association Ltd,
London, in association with Getty Images and
Endeavour London Ltd.

Copyright © 2009 The Reader's Digest Association Ltd

The Reader's Digest Association Ltd
11 Westferry Circus
Canary Wharf
London E14 4HE
www.readersdigest.co.uk

Endeavour London Ltd
21–31 Woodfield Road
London W9 2BA
info@endeavourlondon.com

Written by
Brian Moynahan

For Endeavour
Publisher: Charles Merullo
Designer: Tea Aganovic
Picture editor: Jennifer Jeffrey
Production: Mary Osborne

For Reader's Digest
Project editor: Christine Noble
Art editor: Conorde Clarke
Indexer: Marie Lorimer
Proofreader: Ron Pankhurst
Pre-press account manager: Dean Russell
Product production manager: Claudette Bramble
Production controller: Sandra Fuller

Reader's Digest General Books
Editorial director: Julian Browne
Art director: Anne-Marie Bulat

Colour origination by Chroma Graphics Ltd, Singapore
Printed and bound in China

We are committed both to the quality of our
products and the service we provide to our customers.
We value your comments, so please do contact us on
08705 113366 or via our website at
www.readersdigest.co.uk

If you have any comments or suggestions about
the content of our books, email us at
gbeditorial@readersdigest.co.uk

CONCEPT CODE: UK 0154/L/S
BOOK CODE: 638-006 UP0000-1
ISBN: 978 0 276 44394 7
ORACLE CODE: 356900006H.00.24